Deliverance From The Sin of Gluttony

Practical Helps in Sanctification, Volume 12

Zacharias Tanee Fomum

Published by ZTF Books Online, 2019.

DELIVERANCE FROM THE SIN OF GLUTTONY

First edition. August 11, 2019.

ISBN: 978-1393104780

Written by Zacharias Tanee Fomum.

Table of Contents

I lovingly dedicate this book to

Elisabeth Afor Tanee Fomum,

who does not commit the sin of gluttony.

Preface

This book, *Deliverance from the Sin of Gluttony*, is the seventh book in the series "Practical Helps for Overcomers." The books in the series which have already been written are:

- Book ONE: *Deliverance from Sin*
- Book TWO: *The Way of Sanctification*
- Book THREE: *Sanctified and Consecrated for Spiritual Ministry*
- Book FOUR: *The Seed, the Sower and the Hearts of Men*
- Book FIVE: *Deliverance from the Sin of Adultery and Fornication*
- Book SIX: *You Can Receive a Pure Heart Today*

The sin of gluttony is a serious matter. Due to a lack of teaching, other sins linked to the appetites such as the appetite for sex and alcohol are vigorously condemned when they are abused or when one indulges in them out of God's will. However, the sin of gluttony, which is uncontrolled indulgence in food is hardly ever mentioned. This is very unfortunate. We clearly affirm that the person who commits adultery once and the one who commits gluttony once are both walking in the flesh and are both condemned before God. If there is no place in the kingdom of God for the adulterer or the fornicator who continues in his sin, it is certain that there will be no place in the kingdom of God for the glutton who continues in his sin of gluttony. That being the case, deliverance from the sin of gluttony becomes imperative.

In this book, we are not laying down rules for eating. Neither are we giving practical methods for reducing weight. We are rather showing the way that leads to the Deliverer, the Holy Spirit, for He alone delivers the captives.

May the Lord help you as you read, to enter into freedom from the worship of food, so that you may become a worshipper of the living God.

This is imperative because no glutton can truly worship the living God. He can only be worshipped by people with pure hearts and who are filled with the Holy Spirit. Gluttony prevents one from having a pure heart and from being filled with the Holy Spirit.

We are very conscious of the fact that no one can deliver himself from gluttony. Do not try to set yourself free. If you try, you may succeed for some time however, this success will be short-lived. Surrender yourself along with your problem to the Holy Spirit who lives in you and submit yourself to His treatment. He will succeed and then you too will succeed. You will be set free and your freedom will be permanent.

Praise the Lord!

18th June, 1995.

Zacharias Tanee Fomum

P.O. Box, 6090 Yaounde, Cameroon.

© Zacharias Tanee Fomum.

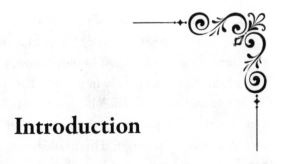

Introduction

I confess that I had wanted to write this book for some time, but the Lord had persistently stood on my way, preventing me from writing it. He wanted to do something in my life before allowing me to write the book or to be more precise, He wanted to do something in my heart so that I become the instrument through which the Blessed Holy Spirit would write the book. During the first hours of this morning, God accomplished in my heart what He wanted. It is not easy to explain it. To put it simply, I received a revelation of a truth which I had known only theoretically for more than twenty years now. That truth, which was revealed to me and which is now my possession, is this; *I know that nothing good lives in me, that is, in my sinful nature. For I have the desire to do what is good, but I cannot carry it out* (Romans 7: 18). I now know deep within me that nothing good lives in Zacharias Tanee Fomum. I now know with certainty that the flesh of Zacharias Tanee Fomum is just as evil as the flesh of the most wicked, the most corrupt, the most desperate and the most helpless sinful person. I know that the flesh of Zacharias Tanee Fomum is capable of committing all sins that human beings have ever committed. I know that the flesh of Zacharias Tanee Fomum and that of the worst thief, the most popular liar, the worst murderer, the worst adulterer, are the same. I now know that the flesh of Zacharias Tanee Fomum is capable of committing the worst kind of murder, the worst kind of adultery, the worst kind of theft, the worst kind of lie, and so on, which have ever been committed. Now I know, I know, I know. I also believe that all the confidence I have in my flesh has ended.

If I had written this book before this day, I would have offered men a series of rules to contribute to what God would do for their deliverance. That would have failed, because it would have led people to take decisions, to be willing, in the flesh; only to realize that they are incapable of accomplishing what they were willing to do. *For I have the desire to do what is good, but I cannot carry it out.*

Now I know that nobody can be delivered from gluttony, which is a work of the flesh, by a fleshly method. I have connected you and I will be connecting you to the Redeemer from the manifestation of the flesh called gluttony. That Redeemer is the Lord Jesus and He alone can set you free. The Lord Jesus says: *...Apart from me you can do nothing* (John 15:5b).

If you know that without the Lord you can do nothing and if you know that you are bound by gluttony and want to be set free, please continue reading. You will get into union with Him and He, by His Holy Spirit, will set you free. The only freedom which is worthy to be received is that which comes from the Lord Jesus. All other redeemers with the supposed deliverance they give are of no avail.

Come with us as we discover together what gluttony is and what must be done to encounter and live in victory with the Redeemer – Jesus Christ.

What Is Gluttony?

GLUTTONY IS GIVING to food the place that has to be given to the Lord God Almighty and to Him alone. It is worshipping food instead of worshipping the Lord God Almighty who alone is to be worshipped.

Gluttony can be manifested in many ways; for instance:

1. Eating what is forbidden
2. Eating more food than is required
3. Refusing to eat a certain type of food
4. An excessive desire to eat a certain type of food.
5. Being excessively strict about the way food is prepared.
6. Being excessively strict on the way food is served.
7. Being excessively strict about meal times.
8. Eating for the pleasure of eating, etc.

The problem with each of these manifestations is that it takes the eyes off the Lord and focuses them on food, such that what was supposed to be a means to an end becomes an end in itself. Gluttony is idolatry. It is the overthrow of God and the enthronement of food in the heart. It is giving to food the love and attention which is to be given to the Lord God Almighty. It is making food: the cooking of food, the eating of food and the enjoyment of food the central issue in life.

God's Plan For Human Nourishment

God's original plan for human nourishment

A nd God saw that the light was good; and God separated the light from the darkness. God called the light Day, and the darkness he called Night. And there was evening and there was morning, one day. And God said, "Let there be a firmament in the midst of the waters, and let it separate the waters from the waters." And God made the firmament and separated the waters which were under the firmament from the waters which were above the firmament. And it was so. And God called the firmament Heaven. And there was evening and there was morning, a second day.

And God said, "Let the waters under the heavens be gathered together into one place, and let the dry land appear." And it was so. God called the dry land Earth, and the waters that were gathered together he called Seas. And God saw that it was good. And God said, "Let the earth put forth vegetation, plants yielding seed, and fruit trees bearing fruit in which is their seed, each according to its kind, upon the earth." And it was so. The earth brought forth vegetation, plants yielding seed according to their own kinds, and trees bearing fruit in which is their seed, each according to its kind. And God saw that it was good. And there was evening and there was morning, a third day.

DELIVERANCE FROM THE SIN OF GLUTTONY

And God said, "Let there be lights in the firmament of the heavens to separate the day from the night; and let them be for signs and for seasons and for days and years, and let them be lights in the firmament of the heavens to give light upon the earth." And it was so. And God made the two great lights, the greater light to rule the day, and the lesser light to rule the night; he made the stars also. And God set them in the firmament of the heavens to give light upon the earth, to rule over the day and over the night, and to separate the light from the darkness. And God saw that it was good. And there was evening and there was morning, a fourth day.

And God said, "Let the waters bring forth swarms of living creatures, and let birds fly above the earth across the firmament of the heavens." So God created the great sea monsters and every living creature that moves, with which the waters swarm, according to their kinds, and every winged bird according to its kind. And God saw that it was good. And God blessed them, saying, "Be fruitful and multiply and fill the waters in the seas, and let birds multiply on the earth." And there was evening and there was morning, a fifth day.

And God said, "Let the earth bring forth living creatures according to their kinds: cattle and creeping things and beasts of the earth according to their kinds." And it was so. And God made the beasts of the earth according to their kinds and the cattle according to their kinds, and everything that creeps upon the ground according to its kind. And God saw that it was good. Then God said, "Let us make man in our image, after our likeness; and let them have dominion over the fish of the sea, and over the birds of the air, and over the cattle, and over all the earth, and over every creeping thing that creeps upon the earth." So God created man in his own image, in the image of God he created him; male and female he created them. And God blessed them, and God said to them, "Be fruitful and multiply, and *fill the earth and subdue it; and have dominion over the fish of the sea and over the birds of the air and over every living thing that moves upon the earth." And God said, "Behold, I have given you every plant yielding seed which is upon the face of all the earth, and every tree with seed in its fruit; you shall have them for food. And to every beast of the earth, and to every bird of the air, and to everything that creeps on the earth, everything that has the breath of life, I have given every green plant for food." And it was so. And God saw everything that he had made, and behold, it was very good. And there was evening and there was morning, a sixth day* (Genesis 1: 4-31, RSV).

God created man.

God gave man a task to accomplish. That task consisted in:

being fruitful,

multiplying,

filling the earth,

subduing the earth,

having dominion over the fish of the sea,

having dominion over the birds of the air and

having dominion over everything that moves on the earth.

The next thing that God did was to provide food for the man He created. The food was to help him be all that God wanted him to be in order to do all that God commanded him to do. So, the food was to help man to be what he had to be in order to accomplish the task God asked him to accomplish for Him.

God could have decided Himself

to subdue the earth,

to have dominion over the fish of the sea,

to have dominion over the birds of the air and

to have dominion over all the animals that move on the earth without the help of man. If He had decided to do things that way, it would have been so and it would have been the direct authority of God subduing the earth, having dominion over the fish of the sea, the birds of the air and over every living thing. If God had decided to work in that manner, He would have done it in all perfection.

However, He did not decide to do things that way. By His own authority, in His indisputable sovereignty, He decided to bring in man. He therefore decided to create man so that man should be His co-worker and become the delegated authority in total submission to Him. The following declaration made by God is pregnant with meaning: *Let us make man in our image, after our likeness; and let them have dominion over the fish of the sea, and over the birds of the air, and over the cattle, and over all the earth, and over every creeping thing that creeps upon the earth* (Genesis 1: 26).

God took the decision to create man so that he should have dominion over the fish of the sea, the birds, the cattle on the earth and the reptiles that move on the earth. Man was established as the supreme authority over the earth; he had to submit only to the supreme authority of the Almighty God.

What an exalted position!

What an honour!

What a responsibility!

What glory!

There is a real sense in which man has to dress according to his responsibility. He has to dress according to who he is, where he is and what he is doing. Anyone who expects that a fisherman entirely occupied in deep sea fishing should dress like an astronaut exploring space is being unreasonable.

In the same wise, it was in the plan of God that eating should be according to who is eating and why he is eating.

God having created man to have such far reaching dominion, gave him the kind of food which was going to best help him to be the best he could in order to function as the master of the earth and over everything in it.

Yes, in order that man should be the best of himself, to have dominion over the fish, the birds, the cattle, over all the creatures and over all the earth, God gave man the following as food: "Every seed-bearing plant on the surface of the whole earth and every tree having fruit with seed in it!"

Man received super abundant provision. He was treated like a boss. He was treated in a super abundant way. Oh! the super abundance of God!

God the First Farmer

THE BIBLE SAYS: *In the day that the LORD God made the earth and the heavens, when no plant of the field was yet in the earth and no herb of the field had yet sprung up - for the LORD God had not caused it to rain upon the earth, and there was no man to till the ground; but a mist went up from the earth and watered the whole face of the ground - then the LORD God formed man of dust from the ground, and breathed into his nostrils the breath of life; and man became a living being. And the LORD God planted a garden in Eden, in the east; and there he put the man whom he had formed. And out of the ground the LORD God made to grow every tree that is pleasant to the sight and good for food, the tree of life also in the midst of the garden, and the tree of the knowledge of good and evil. ... The LORD God took the man and put him in the garden of Eden to till it and keep it.*(Genesis 2: 4-15 RSV).

DELIVERANCE FROM THE SIN OF GLUTTONY

God decided that man needed the best food to keep him in the best health to enable him accomplish the work He had gave him. God moved from decision to action. God planted the first garden. In this garden were all kinds of trees with fruits pleasant to see and good for food.

God gave man the kind of food that was pleasant to see and good for food. It was pleasant to see and nutritious. We can conclude that the food that satisfies God's demand would be pleasant to see and good to eat. It was also abundant and in a varied because the Lord caused many kinds of trees to grow out of the ground.

We conclude that in the original plan of God for human nutrition, He gave to man first class food; that food was from plants, it was abundant and in a great variety. The food was both pleasant to see and good to eat.

The tree of life was also in the Garden of Eden and man could eat of it as well. God's intention was that man should eat of the tree of life and from the other trees in the garden and live eternally on the earth with perpetual strength and perpetual youthfulness in obedience to Him and in communion with Him.

God did not include animals as food for man in his original plan. He neither gave to animals other animals as food. He gave plants as food as well for the animals .

That was God's original plan for the nutrition of man and of animals. It was a plan to ensure that man had the body and the health necessary for him to be what He wanted him to be. It was a plan which enabled the animals to feed without destroying man and without destroying one another. Finally, it was a plan that ensured that man lived eternally.

How wonderful was this plan!

God's Original Plan For Human Nourishment Discarded

Gluttons Of The Bible - 1: The Gluttony Of Adam And Eve

*N*ow *the serpent was more crafty than any of the wild animals the LORD God had made. He said to the woman, "Did God really say, "You must not eat from any tree in the garden?"*

The woman said to the serpent, "We may eat fruit from the trees in the garden, but God did say, 'You must not eat fruit from the tree that is in the middle of the garden, and you must not touch it, or you will die.'"

"You will not surely die," the serpent said to the woman. "For God knows that when you eat of it your eyes will be opened, and you will be like God, knowing good and evil."

When the woman saw that the fruit of the tree was good for food and pleasing to the eyes, and also desirable for gaining wisdom, she took some and ate it. She also gave some to her husband, who was with her, and he ate it. Then the eyes of both of them were opened, and they realized that they were naked; so they sewed fig leaves together and made coverings for themselves.

DELIVERANCE FROM THE SIN OF GLUTTONY

Then the man and his wife heard the sound of the LORD God as he was walking in the garden in the cool of the day, and they hid from the LORD God among the trees of the garden. But the LORD God called to the man, "Where are you?"

He answered, "I heard you in the garden and I was afraid because I was naked; so I hid."

And he said, "Who told you that you were naked? Have you eaten from the tree from which I commanded you not to eat?"

The man said, "The woman you put here with me – she gave me some fruit from the tree and I ate it."

Then the LORD God said to the woman, "What is this you have done?"

The woman said, "The serpent deceived me, and I ate."

So the LORD God said to the serpent, "Because you have done this, cursed are you above all the livestock and all the wild animals! You will crawl on your belly and you will eat dust all the days of your life. And I will put enmity between you and the woman, and between your offspring and hers: he will crush your head, and you will strike his heel."

To the woman he said, "I will greatly increase your pains in childbearing; with pain you will give birth to children. Your desire will be for your husband, and he will rule over you."

To Adam he said, "Because you listened to your wife and ate from the tree about which I commanded you, 'You must not eat of it,' "Cursed is the ground because of you: through painful toil you will eat of it all the days of your life. It will produce thorns and thistles for you and you will eat the plants of the field. By the sweat of your brow you will eat your food until you return to the ground, since from it you were taken; for dust you are and to dust you will return."

Adam named his wife Eve because she would become the mother of all the living.

The LORD God made garments of skin for Adam and his wife and clothed them. And the LORD God said, "The man has now become like one of us, knowing good and evil. He must not be allowed to reach out his hand and take also from the tree of life and eat and live forever." So the Lord God banished him from the Garden of Eden to work the ground from which he had been taken. After he drove the man out, he placed on the east side of the Garden of Eden cherubim and a flaming sword flashing back and forth to guard the way to the tree of life Genesis 3: 1-24).

God provided Adam and Eve with an enormous variety of trees whose fruits were all pleasing to look at and good for food. All their desires could be met. There were so many trees of pleasing appearance and that were sources of exceptional food that Adam and Eve had not even tasted of, to know what they offered. The tree of life was in the garden. Its fruits were good to look at and it was nutritive and gave life. Adam and Eve had not yet enjoyed its fruit!

Adam and Eve had heard what God said: *You are free to eat from any tree in the garden; but you must not eat from the tree of the knowledge of good and evil, for when you eat of it you will surely die* (Genesis 2: 16-17).

They could eat of all the trees except one! They could eat of the tree of life. God was not over-restrictive. They were forbidden one tree out of thousands or millions.

The serpent caused Adam and Eve to commit the sin of gluttony by eating the fruit of the only tree that God forbade. This tree had two properties in common with all the other trees: it was good for food and it was pleasing to the eye. It had one property that was uniquely its own: it was desirable for gaining wisdom. Adam and Eve wanted wisdom from a source that was not of God. They committed gluttony in order to gain forbidden wisdom. They were to deny themselves and reject a wisdom that was offered by a person and a source that was not of God. They refused to deny themselves this illegal wisdom. Rather, they chose to gratify themselves with God-forbidden wisdom. That was sin – gluttony, disobedience, independence, self-gratification!

That sin earned them separation from God and physical death!

Gluttony always separates from God and brings physical death!

So far-reaching was the sin of Adam and Eve that it affected all humanity and all the earth! The serpent was punished! There was warfare installed between the serpent and the woman, between the offspring of the serpent and the offspring of the woman. This enmity continues until today! You know how you react at the sight of a serpent! The abundance was restricted because the ground was cursed. The ground was doomed to produce thorns and thistles for man to grapple with! The whole earth knew a curse that even in our day is manifested in earthquakes, eruptions and all the other phenomena that make the earth an unpleasant habitation to man!

Adam and Eve died before the first day of God (one thousand years) was over and since then no one has ever lived more than one God-day (A God-day is one thousand years (2Peter 3:8)!

God's Modified Plan For Human Nourishment

THIS IS THE WRITTEN account of Adam's line.

When God created man, he made him in the likeness of God. He created them male and female and blessed them. And when they were created, he called them "man".

When Adam had lived 130 years, he had a son in his own likeness, in his own image; and he named him Seth. After Seth was born, Adam lived 800 years and had other sons and daughters. Altogether, Adam lived 930 years and then he died.

When Seth had lived 105 years, he became the father of Enosh. And after he became the father of Enosh, Seth lived 807 years and had other sons and daughters. Altogether, Seth lived 912 years, and then he died.

When Enosh had lived 90 years, he became the father of Kenan. And after he became the father of Kenan, Enosh lived 815 years and had other sons and daughters. Altogether, Enosh lived 905 years, and then he died.

When Kenan had lived 70 years, he became the father of Mahalalel. And after he became the father of Mahalalel, Kenan lived 840 years and had other sons and daughters. Altogether, Kenan lived 910 years, and then he died.

When Mahalalel had lived 65 years, he became the father of Jared. And after he became the father of Jared, Mahalalel lived 830 years and had other sons and daughters. Altogether, Mahalalel lived 895 years, and then he died.

When Jared had lived 162 years, he became the father of Enoch. And after he became the father of Enoch, Jared lived 800 years and had other sons and daughters. Altogether, Jared lived 962 years, and then he died.

When Enoch had lived 65 years, he became the father of Methuselah. And after he became the father of Methuselah, Enoch walked with God 300 years and had other sons and daughters. Altogether, Enoch lived 365 years. Enoch walked with God; then he was no more, because God took him away.

DELIVERANCE FROM THE SIN OF GLUTTONY

When Methuselah had lived 187 years, he became the father of Lamech. And after he became the father of Lamech, Methuselah lived 782 years and had other sons and daughters. Altogether, Methuselah lived 969 years, and then he died.

When Lamech had lived 182 years, he had a son. He named him Noah and said, "He will comfort us in the labour and painful toil of our hands caused by the ground the Lord has cursed." After Noah was born, Lamech lived 595 years and had other sons and daughters. Altogether, Lamech lived 777 years, and then he died.

After Noah was 500 years old, he became the father of Shem, Ham and Japheth (Genesis 5:1-32).

When men began to increase in number on the earth and daughters were born to them, the sons of God saw that the daughters of men were beautiful, and they married any of them they chose. Then the Lord said, "My Spirit will not contend with man forever, for he is mortal; his days will be a hundred and twenty years" (Genesis 6:1-3).

Then God blessed Noah and his sons, saying to them, "Be fruitful and increase in number and fill the earth. The fear and dread of you will fall upon all the beasts of the earth and all the birds of the air, upon every creature that moves along the ground, and upon all the fish of the sea; they are given into your hands. Everything that lives and moves will be food for you. Just as I gave you the green plants, I now give you everything (Genesis 9: 1-3).

Although Adam and Eve sinned and God let them have the death that they deserved, man continued to live for many hundreds of years. This can be seen in Adam (930 years), Seth (912 years); Enosh (905 years), Kenan (910 years), Mahalalel (895 years), Jared (962 years), Methuselah (969 years), Lamech (777years).

There was the sinful marriage between the sons of God and the daughters of men (sinful because it was not authored by God but by men). God was so offended by this that he decreed: *My spirit will not contend with man forever, for he is corrupt; his days will be a hundred and twenty* (Genesis 6: 3).

By the time this decree was passed by God, Noah had clocked 500 years!- and had had three sons.

The new decree was pronounced upon fallen man. It was necessary for him to have a new diet– one that would suit a frame that would live for 120 years. For that diet, God said to Noah," *Be fruitful and increase in number and fill the earth. The fear and dread of you will fall upon all the beasts of the earth and all the birds of the air, upon every creature that moves along the ground, and upon all the fish of the sea; they are given into your hands. Everything that lives and moves will be food for you. Just as I gave you the green plants, I now give you everything"* (Genesis 9:1-3).

The food for fallen man is as follows: everything that lives and everything that moves; all the animals, and all the plants; all the insects and all the sea creatures. All have been given to man for food.

This offer of all for food implies that to reject something that God has made and which can be eaten as food and which is being eaten as food by some human beings is wrong. It is the despising of some food and the exalting of other types of food. This is a form of gluttony. The Apostle Peter was once caught in this. The Bible says, *About noon the following day as they were on their journey and approaching the city, Peter went up on the roof to pray. He became hungry and wanted something to eat, and while the meal was being prepared, he fell into a trance. He saw heaven opened and something like a large sheet being let down to earth by its four corners. It contained all kinds of four-footed animals, as well as reptiles of the earth and birds of the air. Then a voice told him, "Get up, Peter.*

Kill and eat" "Surely not, Lord!" Peter replied. *"I have never eaten anything impure or unclean." The voice spoke to him a second time, "Do not call anything impure that God has made clean." This happened three times, and immediately the sheet was taken back to heaven* (Acts 10: 9-16).

God has made all animals and plants clean and good for food. To reject some and prefer others is a form of idolatry of food – the worship of some types of food and the despising of others.

The Lord Jesus told the seventy-two that he sent out to preach the Gospel, *Stay in that house, eating and drinking whatever they give you, for the worker deserves his wages. Do not move around from house to house* (Luke 10: 7). The words, *"Eating and drinking whatever they give you"* imply that the worker was to have no choices. All that the people ate could be eaten by him without harm.

We conclude by saying that in the modified plan of God, plants and animals are to be eaten. They are to be accepted as God-given food. God has not called people living after the fall to be vegetarians only unless they cannot provide for meat by honest ways. God expects His children to eat meat as well as vegetables. The vegetarian is not living a more consecrated life than the one who eats meat. The vegetarian who can have meat but would not eat it is not superior spiritually. He is one with a weak faith who should be permitted to eat as he has chosen!

God's Modified Plan For Human Nourishment Fulfilled In The Life Of Jehoiada.

In the seventh year Jehoiada showed his strength. He made a covenant with the commanders of units of a hundred: Azariah son of Jeroham, Ishmael son of Jehohanan, Azariah son of Obed, Maaseiah son of Adaiah, and Elishaphat son of Zicri. They went throughout Judah and gathered the Levites and the heads of Israelite families from all the towns. When they came to Jerusalem, the whole assembly made a covenant with the king at the temple of God. Jehoiada said to them, "The king's son shall reign, as the LORD promised concerning the descendants of David. Now this is what you are to do: A third of you priests and Levites who are going on duty on the Sabbath are to keep watch at the doors, a third of you at the royal palace and a third at the Foundation Gate, and all the other men are to be in the courtyards of the temple of the LORD. No one is to enter the temple of the LORD except the priests and Levites on duty; they may enter because they are consecrated, but all the other men are to guard what the LORD has assigned to them. The Levites are to station themselves around the king, each man with his weapons in his hand. Anyone who enters the temple must be put to death. Stay close to the king wherever he goes."

The Levites and all the men of Judah did just as Jehoiada the priest ordered. Each one took his men—those who were going on duty on the Sabbath and those who were going off duty—for Jehoiada the priest had not released any of the divisions. Then he gave the commanders of units of a hundred the spears and the large and small shields that had belonged to King David and that were in the temple of God. He stationed all the men, each with his weapon in his hand, around the king—near the altar and the temple, from the south side to the north side of the temple.

Jehoiada and his sons brought out the king's son and put the crown on him; they presented him with a copy of the covenant and proclaimed him king. They anointed him and shouted, "Long live the king!"

When Athaliah heard the noise of the people running and cheering the king, she went to them at the temple of the LORD. She looked, and there was the king, standing by his pillar at the entrance. The officers and the trumpeters were beside the king, and all the people of the land were rejoicing and blowing trumpets, and singers with musical instruments were leading the praises. Then Athaliah tore her robes and shouted, "Treason! Treason!"

Jehoiada the priest sent out the commanders of units of a hundred, who were in charge of the troops, and said to them: "Bring her out between the ranks and put to the sword anyone who follows her." For the priest had said, "Do not put her to death at the temple of the LORD." So they seized her as she reached the entrance of the Horse Gate on the palace grounds, and there they put her to death.

Jehoiada then made a covenant that he and the people and the king would be the LORD's people. All the people went to the temple of Baal and tore it down. They smashed the altars and idols and killed Mattan the priest of Baal in front of the altars.

Then Jehoiada placed the oversight of the temple of the LORD in the hands of the priests, who were Levites, to whom David had made assignments in the temple, to present the burnt offerings of the LORD as written in the Law of Moses, with rejoicing and singing, as David had ordered. He also stationed doorkeepers at the gates of the LORD's temple so that no one who was in any way unclean might enter. He took with him the commanders of hundreds, the nobles, the rulers of

*the people and all the people of the land and brought the king down
from the temple of the LORD. They went into the palace through the
Upper Gate and seated the king on the royal throne,*

*and all the people of the land rejoiced. And the city was quiet,
because Athaliah had been slain with the sword.*

*Joash was seven years old when he became king, and he reigned
in Jerusalem forty years. His mother's name was Zibiah; she was from
Beersheba. Joash did what was right in the eyes of the LORD all the
years of Jehoiada the priest. Jehoiada chose two wives for him, and he
had sons and daughters.*

*Some time later Joash decided to restore the temple of the LORD.
He called together the priests and Levites and said to them, "Go to the
towns of Judah and collect the money due annually from all Israel, to
repair the temple of your God. Do it now." But the Levites did not act
at once.*

*Therefore the king summoned Jehoiada the chief priest and said to
him, "Why haven't you required the Levites to bring in from Judah
and Jerusalem the tax imposed by Moses the servant of the LORD and
by the assembly of Israel for the Tent of the Testimony?" Now the sons
of that wicked woman Athaliah had broken into the temple of God
and had used even its sacred objects for the Baals.*

*At the king's command, a chest was made and placed outside, at
the gate of the temple of the LORD. A proclamation was then issued
in Judah and Jerusalem that they should bring to the LORD the tax
that Moses the servant of God had required of Israel in the desert.
All the officials and all the people brought their contributions gladly,
dropping them into the chest until it was full.*

*Whenever the chest was brought in by the Levites to the king's
officials and they saw that there was a large amount of money, the
royal secretary and the officer of the chief priest would come and empty*

the chest and carry it back to its place. They did this regularly and collected a great amount of money. The king and Jehoiada gave it to the men who carried out the work required for the temple of the LORD. They hired masons and carpenters to restore the LORD's temple, and also workers in iron and bronze to repair the temple.

The men in charge of the work were diligent, and the repairs progressed under them. They rebuilt the temple of God according to its original design and reinforced it. When they had finished, they brought the rest of the money to the king and Jehoiada, and with it were made articles for the LORD's temple: articles for the service and for the burnt offerings, and also dishes and other objects of gold and silver. As long as Jehoiada lived, burnt offerings were presented continually in the temple of the LORD.

Now Jehoiada was old and full of years, and he died at the age of a hundred and thirty. He was buried with the kings in the City of David, because of the good he had done in Israel for God and his temple (2 Chronicles 23: 1-21; 24:1-16).

The Lord reduced man's life span to 120 years. Jehoiada walked with God and worked for God. He ate like other people and God blessed him with an extra ten years beyond the 120.

God can do that again. Moses lived to be 120 and still had excellent sight. Had he not sinned, he would have lived more than 120 years.

People who walk with God in holiness and in spiritual service should look to the Lord and believe the Lord to enable them to live disease-free lives, full of usefulness to God and His people up to the age of 120 and perhaps more.

What He did for Jehoiada, He can do for you! Glory be to His holy name!

Gluttons of The Bible

The Gluttony Of Esau

This is the account of Abraham's son Isaac.

Abraham became the father of Isaac, and Isaac was forty years old when he married Rebekah daughter of Bethuel the Aramean from Paddan Aram and sister of Laban the Aramean.

Isaac prayed to the Lord on behalf of his wife, because she was barren. The Lord answered his prayer, and his wife Rebekah became pregnant. The babies jostled each other within her, and she said, "Why is this happening to me?" So she went to enquire of the Lord.

The Lord said to her, "Two nations are in your womb, and two peoples from within you will be separated; one people will be stronger than the other, and the older will serve the younger."

When the time came for her to give birth, there were twin boys in her womb. The first to come out was red, and his whole body was like a hairy garment; so they named him Esau. After this, his brother came out, with his hand grasping Esau's heel; so he was named Jacob. Isaac was sixty years old when Rebekah gave birth to them.

The boys grew up, and Esau became a skilful hunter, a man of the open country, while Jacob was a quiet man, staying among the tents. Isaac, who had a taste for wild game, loved Esau, but Rebekah loved Jacob.

DELIVERANCE FROM THE SIN OF GLUTTONY

Once when Jacob was cooking some stew, Esau came in from the open country, famished. He said to Jacob, "Quick, let me have some of that red stew! I'm famished!" (That is why he was also called Edom.) Jacob replied, "First sell me your birthright."

"Look, I am about to die," Esau said. "What good is the birthright to me?"

But Jacob said, "Swear to me first." So he swore an oath to him, selling his birthright to Jacob.

Then Jacob gave Esau some bread and some lentil stew. He ate and drank, and then got up and left. So Esau despised his birthright (Genesis 25:19-34).

Esau was the first born. He was consequently the one to receive the blessings of the elder son. This would have made him one of the Patriarchs. God would have called Himself "The God of Abraham, Isaac and Esau."

Unfortunately, Esau lost all this because of a single meal. It is true that he was hungry but he ought to have controlled himself. He heard his brother say, "First sell me your birthright," yet he took things lightly. He even said, "I am about to die. What good is the birthright to me?" His brother pressed hard and said, "Swear to me first." Esau still refused to confront the gravity of the situation. He swore an oath to Jacob, selling his birthright to him. After he had sold it, he was treated to a good meal – bread, lentil stew and drink. He had thus demoted himself by personal choice. He made food his god and feared rather mistakenly that he would die if he did not eat at once!

Make every effort to live in peace with all men and to be holy; without holiness no one will see the Lord. See, to it that no one misses the grace of God and that no bitter root grows up to cause trouble and defile many. See that no one is sexually immoral, or is godless like

Esau, who for a single meal sold his inheritance rights as the oldest son. Afterwards, as you know, when he wanted to inherit this blessing, he was rejected. He could bring about no change of mind, though he sought the blessing with tears (Hebrews 12:14-17).

Esau is here described as godless. He actually had one god – his belly and he served and worshipped that god faithfully. He sacrificed everything in the service of the god, food. He sold so much for so little.

It was just one meal, but he yielded and it cost him dearly.

Esau afterwards wanted to inherit what the older of the sons was to inherit. He gave away his birthright and somehow thought he could still have it back!

God is not mocked! What a man sows, that he will reap! Small decisions could have far-reaching consequences. There are choices to make and every person is what he is today as a result of the choices he has made all along. What he will be tomorrow is being determined by the choices that are being made today.

Someone may be telling you, "Take an extra piece! It won't hurt!" The truth is that it will hurt. It will hurt your relationship with the Holy Spirit. When he has blown His whistle, saying that you have had enough, every piece, slice, sip taken after that is disobedience. It is gluttony and you will not be quite the same after you have disobeyed Him and eaten that extra slice or piece. Disobedience, even the slightest, means that your fellowship with Him is immediately broken. Do you know what that short time of broken fellowship might cost you? It could cost you your physical life. It could also cost you your ministry, your everything.

Esau lost everything by choosing a meal instead of his birthright. Have you given away your place in God's heart because of a spoonful of rice; a piece of meat and some other food? If you have, please go back to Him in repentance. He will have compassion on you, forgive you and give you another opportunity. Do not give up!

The Gluttony Of Isaac

WHEN ISAAC WAS OLD and his eyes were so weak that he could no longer see, he called for Esau his older son and said to him, "My son."

"Here I am," he answered.

Isaac said, "I am now an old man and don't know the day of my death. Now then, get your weapons – your quiver and bow – and go to the open country to hunt some wild game for me. Prepare me the kind of tasty food I like and bring it to me to eat, so that I may give you my blessing before I die."

Now Rebekah was listening as Isaac spoke to his son Esau. When Esau left for the open country to hunt game and bring it back, Rebekah said to her son Jacob, "Look, I overheard your father say to your brother Esau, 'Bring me some game and prepare me some tasty food to eat, so that I may give you my blessing in the presence of the Lord before I die.' Now, my son, listen carefully and do what I tell you: Go out to the flock and bring me two choice young goats, so that I can prepare some tasty food for your father, just the way he likes it. Then take it to your father to eat, so that he may give you his blessing before he dies."

Jacob said to Rebekah his mother, "But my brother Esau is a hairy man, and I'm a man with smooth skin. What if my father touches me? I would appear to be tricking him and would bring a curse on myself rather than a blessing."

His mother said to him, "My son, let the curse fall on me. Just do what I say; go and get them for me."

So he went and got them and brought them to his mother, and she prepared some tasty food, just the way his father liked it. Then Rebekah took the best clothes of Esau her older son, which she had in the house, and put on her younger son Jacob. She also covered his hands and the sooth part of his neck with the goatskins. Then she handed to her son Jacob the tasty food and the bread she had made.

He went to his father and said, "My father."

"Yes, my son," he answered. "Who is it?"

Jacob said to his father, "I am Esau your firstborn, I have done as you told me. Please sit up and eat some of my game so that you may give me your blessing."

Isaac asked his son, "How did you find it so quickly, my son?"

"The Lord your God gave me success," he replied.

Then Isaac said to Jacob, "Come near so that I can touch you, my son, to know whether you really are my son Esau or not."

Jacob went close to his father Isaac, who touched him and said, "The voice is the voice of Jacob, but the hands are the hands of Esau." He did not recognize him, for his hands were hairy like those of his brother Esau; so he blessed him. "Are you really my son Esau?" he asked.

"I am," he replied.

Then he said, "My son, bring me some of your game to eat, so that I may give you my blessing."

Jacob brought it to him and he ate: and he brought some wine and he drank. Then his father Isaac said to him, "Come here, my son, and kiss me.'

So he went to him and kissed him. When Isaac caught the smell of his clothes, he blessed him and said,

DELIVERANCE FROM THE SIN OF GLUTTONY

"Ah, the smell of my son is like the smell of a field that the Lord has blessed. May God give you of heaven's dew and of earth's richness—and abundance of grain and new wine May nations serve you and peoples bow down to you. Be lord over your brothers, and may the sons of your mother bow down to you. May those who curse you be cursed and those who bless you be blessed."

After Isaac finished blessing him and Jacob had scarcely left his father's presence, his brother Esau came in from hunting. He too prepared some tasty food and brought it to his father. Then he said to him, "My father, sit up and eat some of my game, so that you may give me your blessing."

His father Isaac asked him, "Who are you?"

"I am your son," he answered, "your firstborn, Esau."

Isaac trembled violently and said, "Who was it, then, that hunted game and brought it to me? I ate it just before you came and I blessed him—and indeed he will be blessed!"

When Esau heard his father's words he burst out with a loud and bitter cry and said to his father, "Bless me – me too, my father!"

But he said, "Your brother came deceitfully and took your blessing."

Esau said, "Isn't he rightly named Jacob? He has deceived me these two times: He took my birthright, and now he's taken my blessing!" Then he asked, "Haven't you reserved any blessing for me?"

Isaac answered Esau, "I have made him lord over you and have made all his relatives his servants, and I have sustained him with grain and new wine. So what can I possibly do for you, my son?"

Esau said to his father, "Do you have only one blessing, my father? Bless me too, my father!" Then Esau wept aloud.

His father Isaac answered him, "Your dwelling will be away from the earth's richness, away from the dew of heaven above. You will live by the sword and you will serve your brother. But when you grow restless, you will throw his yoke from off your neck" (Genesis 27:1-40).

When Isaac was old, he began to lose his physical vision. He probably also began to lose his spiritual vision, for he specialized in eating wild game. He intended to bless his older son, but he demanded that he should bring him the kind of tasty food that he liked before he did this. His words to Esau were, "I am now an old man and don't know the day of my death. Now then, get your weapons – your quiver and bow – and go to the open country to hunt some wild game for me. Prepare me the kind of tasty food that I like and bring it to me to eat, so that I may give you my blessing before I die." When a man of consequence demands that tasty food be brought to him to eat before he blesses a son, he makes himself a glutton by trying very far-reaching issues to his appetites.

When Jacob brought the food that Rebekah had prepared and invited him to eat it, he was suspicious of the person bringing the food. He said, "Come near so that I can touch you, my son, to know whether you really are my son Esau or not."

When Isaac touched him, he said, "The voice is the voice of Jacob, but the hands are those of Esau." This was a point at which, were he not given to food he would have waited and called for others to help him to discern. Unfortunately, the desire to eat the tasty meat was on his heart and he would neither wait nor call for help for further evidence. He merely asked a flimsy question "Are you really my son Esau?" To this, Jacob answered, "I am." That settled all as far as he was concerned. He let go the matter of the conflict as to whose voice it was and asked for the food.

Although he had eaten wild game for much of his life, he ate goat meat and was so taken up with it that he thought it was wild game.

DELIVERANCE FROM THE SIN OF GLUTTONY

After he had eaten and drunk, he blessed Jacob, thinking that he was blessing Esau.

Isaac was a meat glutton. Can you imagine that he alone ate two young goats in one meal?

Gluttons give the place to food that ought to be given to God! When it was time to bless one of his sons and make him greater than the other, Isaac did not take up the matter with God. He took the matter up with his stomach and his taste buds, and that is tragic!

Are you giving to your stomach the place that you ought to give to God?

Are you giving to your taste buds; the place that you ought to give to God?

Are you being deceived by food?

Are your choices being governed by the availability of choice food?

Is your choice being determined by the capacity to cook the type of food that you like?

Are you giving away so much for so little?

May the Lord deliver you from the love of tasty food.

May the Lord deliver you from the love of meat.

May all foods be lawful to you and may none control you, making you its slave.

May you maintain the spiritual vigour of your youthful days until the coming of the Lord.

God bless you!

The Gluttony Of The Children Of Israel In The Wilderness-1

NOW THE PEOPLE COMPLAINED about their hardships in the hearing of the Lord, and when he heard them his anger was aroused. Then fire from the LORD burned among them and consumed some of the outskirts of the camp. When the people cried out to Moses, he prayed to the LORD and the fire died down. So that place was called Taberah, because fire from the LORD had burned among them.

The rabble with them began to crave other food, and again the Israelites started wailing and said, "If only we had meat to eat! We remember the fish we ate in Egypt at no cost – also the cucumbers, melons, leeks, onions and garlic. But now we have lost our appetite; we never see anything but this manna!"

The manna was like coriander seed and looked like resin. The people went around gathering it, and then ground it in a hand mill or crushed it in a mortar. They cooked it in a pot or made it into cakes. And it tasted like something made with olive oil. When the dew settled on the camp at night, the manna also came down.

Moses heard the people of every family wailing, each at the entrance to his tent. The Lord became exceedingly angry, and Moses was troubled. He asked the LORD, "Why have you brought this trouble on your servant? What have I done to displease you that you put the burden of all these people on me? Did I conceive all these people? Did I give them birth? Why do you tell me to carry them in my arms as a nurse carries an infant, to the land you promised on oath to their forefathers? Where can I get meat for all these people? They keep wailing to me, 'Give us meat to eat!' I cannot carry all these people by myself; the burden is too heavy for me. If this is how you are going to treat me, put me to death right now – if I have found favour in your eyes – and do not let me face my own ruin."

The LORD said to Moses, "Bring me seventy of Israel's elders who are known to you as leaders and officials among the people. Make them come to the Tent of Meeting that they may stand there with you. I will come down and speak with you there, and I will take of the Spirit that is on you and put the Spirit on them. They will help you carry the burden of the people so that you will not have to carry it alone.

Tell the people: 'Consecrate yourselves in preparation for tomorrow, when you will eat meat. The LORD heard you when you wailed, "If only we had meat to eat! We were better off in Egypt!" Now the Lord will give you meat, and you will eat it. You will not eat it for just one day, or two days, or five, ten or twenty days, but for a whole month – until it comes out of your nostrils and you loathe it – because you have rejected the Lord, who is among you, and have wailed before him saying, "Why did we ever leave Egypt?"

But Moses said, "Here I am among six hundred thousand men on foot, and you say, 'I will give them meat to eat for a whole month! Would they have enough if flocks and herds were slaughtered for them? Would they have enough if all the fish in the sea were caught for them?"

The LORD answered Moses, "Is the Lord's arm too short? You will now see whether or not what I say will come true for you."

So Moses went out and told the people what the LORD had said. He brought together seventy of the elders and made them stand round the Tent. Then the LORD came down in the cloud and spoke with him, and he took of the Spirit that was on him and put the Spirit on the seventy elders. When the Spirit rested on them, they prophesied, but they did not do so again.

However, two men, whose names were Eldad and Medad, had remained in the camp. They were listed among the elders, but did not go out to the Tent. Yet the Spirit also rested on them, and they prophesied in the camp. A young man ran and told Moses, "Eldad and Medad are prophesying in the camp."

Joshua son of Nun, who had been Moses' assistant since youth, spoke up and said, "Moses, my lord, stop them!"

But Moses replied, "Are you jealous for my sake? I wish that all the Lord's people were prophets and that the LORD would pour his Spirit on them!" Then Moses and the elders of Israel returned to the camp.

Now a wind went out from the LORD and drove quails in from the sea. It brought them down all around the camp to about three feet above the ground, as far as a day's walk in any direction. All that day and night and all the next day the people went out and gathered quail. No one gathered less than ten homers. Then they spread them out all around the camp. But while the meat was still between their teeth and before it could be consumed, the anger of the LORD burned against the people, and he struck them with a severe plague. Therefore the place was named Kibroth Hattaavah because there they buried the people who had craved other food (Numbers 11: 1-34).

The Israelites were in Egypt as part of God's purpose for them. When God's time for their being in Egypt was over, He brought them out so that they might settle in their own land. On their way, God gave them the food that He knew they needed. He gave them the food He Himself prepared from heaven – manna. It contained all that they needed for their bodies – carbohydrates, proteins, vitamins, fats, mineral salts and all else. It was provided on a daily basis and it was abundant. It met all their real needs except for an unholy desire for variety.

It should be noted that it was the rabble (the mixed multitude of non-Israelites who came out with the Israelites) that began to crave other foods. The rabble started and the Israelites followed and started wailing and said, *"If only we had meat to eat! We remember the fish we ate in Egypt at no cost – also the cucumbers, melons, leeks, onions and garlic. But we have lost our appetite; we never see anything but this manna"*

They were discontent.

They wanted variety.

They were not in need of food to feed their bodies for the job of the moment; that, God gave them in abundance. They wanted luxuries!

Those who want the food that they need to accomplish God's call on their lives should ask Him and He will give them. Those who are discontent with God's gracious provisions and draw up a long list of all the extras that He must provide to meet their wants and their desires for excesses will get into trouble with God.

Spiritual people ask the Lord for their needs.

Carnal people ask the Lord for their needs, wants, luxurious and excesses!

These people were not content to be in God's programme. They wished they were in Egypt because of the wide variety of foods! They despised God's provision!

God gave them meat in His displeasure. He gave them meat for one month in His displeasure. The Lord said, *Now the Lord will give you meat, and you will eat it. You will not eat it for just one day or two days or five, ten or twenty days, but for a whole month – until it comes out of your nostrils and you loathe it – because you have rejected the Lord, who is among you, and have wailed before him saying. "Why did we ever leave Egypt?"* (Numbers 11: 18c-20).

The Lord gave them meat for one month! It was meat given in His hot displeasure. The Bible says, *But while the meat was still between their teeth and before it could be consumed, the anger of the Lord burned against the people, and he struck them with a severe plague* (Numbers 11:33).

Uncontrolled appetites are dangerous. God has promised that He will feed us. He says, *So do not worry, saying, 'What shall we eat?' or 'What shall we drink?' or 'What shall we wear?' For the pagans run after all these things, and your heavenly Father knows that you need them. But seek first his kingdom and his righteousness, and all these things will be given to you as well* (Matthew 6: 31-33).

Some people, in obedience to the above call, made it their priority business to seek first the Lord's kingdom and his righteousness. They were so preoccupied with this that they had no time to invest into asking for their food and clothing. However, the Lord who knows their needs in food and clothing supplied these to them even without their asking!

The problem with many of God's children is that they are so taken up with food and clothing and with prayers and prayers about food and clothing that they have no time for God's priorities of His kingdom and His righteousness!

This is a great pity.

The fact that the Israelites who craved meat were punished should stand as a warning to us. Those of God's children who crave this thing and that thing; this food and that food; this food prepared this way and this food prepared that way, and so on, may not go unpunished.

God may punish them by withdrawing from them a hunger for spiritual food.

Is that what has happened to you? Will you repent and cry out to God for mercy?

The Gluttony Of The Children Of Israel In The Wilderness - 2

WHEN THE CANAANITE king of Arad, who lived in the Negev, heard that Israel was coming along the road to Atharim, he attacked the Israelites and captured some of them. Then Israel made this vow to the Lord, "If you will deliver these people into our hands, we will totally destroy their cities." The Lord listened to Israel's plea and gave the Canaanites over to them. They completely destroyed them and their towns; so the place was named Hormah.

They travelled from Mount Hor along the route to the Red Sea, to go round Edom. But the people grew impatient on the way; they spoke against God and against Moses, and said, "Why have you brought us up out of Egypt to die in the desert? There is no bread! There is no water! And we detest this miserable food!"

Then the Lord sent venomous snakes among them; they bit the people and many Israelites died. The people came to Moses and said, "We sinned when we spoke against the Lord and against you. Pray that the Lord will take the snakes away from us." So Moses prayed for the people.

The Lord said to Moses, "Make a snake and put it up on a pole: anyone who is bitten can look at it and live." So Moses made a bronze snake and put it on a pole. Then when anyone was bitten by a snake and looked at the bronze snake, he lived.

The Israelites moved on and camped at Oboth. Then they set out from Oboth and camped in the Abarim in the desert that faces Moab towards the sunrise. From there they moved on and camped in the Zered Valley. They set out from there and camped alongside the Arnon, which is in the desert extending into Amorite territory. The Arnon is the border of Moab, between Moab and the Amorites. That is why the Book of the Wars of the Lord says:

"... Waheb in Suphah and the ravines,
The Arnon and the slopes of the ravines
that lead to the site, of Ar
and lie along the border on Moab."

From there they continued on to Beer, the well where the Lord said to Moses, "Gather the people together and I will give them water."

Then Israel sang this song:

"Spring up, O well!
Sing about it,
about the well that the princes dug
that the nobles of the people sank
the nobles with sceptres and staffs."

Then they went from the desert to Mattanah, from Mattanah to Nahaliel, from Nahaliel to Bamoth, and from Bamoth to the valley in Moab where the top of Pisgah overlooks the wasteland (Numbers 21: 1-20).

The Israelites again complained against God and Moses and said, "Why have you brought us up out of Egypt to die in the desert? There is no bread! There is no water! And we detest this miserable food!"

The food was good enough for their soldiers enabling them to be strong enough to destroy their enemies. It must have been very good. However, they called it miserable food!

It was not the food that was miserable. Food cannot be miserable. It was the people who were miserable. Miserable people despise God's blessings and seek something else, or they seek other things!

They were ungrateful.

Worshippers of food often complain when some aspect of their diet is not provided to them.

Are you prone to complaining?

Do you complain about food? If you do, you should watch out! You may also be complaining about your political leaders,

> your spiritual leaders,
> your partner,
> your children,
> your servant or boss,
> your car,
> your chairs,
> your job
> the telephone system,
> the electricity supply,
> the water supply,
> the roads,
> the weather,
> the postal system,
> the banking system,
> clothes,
> shoes,
> chairs,
> bed,
> cupboard,
> plates,
> the sun,

the moon,
the wind,
and others.

A complaining heart is one that lacks God. Because God has not been given His place in that life, there is a vacuum that opens the way to the flow of complaints.

If yours is a murmuring, grumbling and complaining heart, you have lost God! Rush back to Him. The answer to your complaining is not that you be given the thing you are complaining about. That thing will not satisfy because after you have received it, you will complain about another thing or about other things. Get back to God. Be filled with Him and your complaints will end.

God bless you!

The Disqualification Of The Twenty-One Thousand Seven Hundred Soldiers At The Water

EARLY IN THE MORNING, Jerub-Baal (that is, Gideon) and all his men camped at the spring of Harod. The camp of Midian was north of them in the valley near the hill of Moreh. The LORD said to Gideon, "You have too many men for me to deliver Midian into their hands. In order that Israel may not boast against me that her own strength has saved her, announce now to the people, 'Anyone who trembles with fear may turn back and leave Mount Gilead.'" So twenty-two thousand men left, while ten thousand remained.

But the LORD said to Gideon, "There are still too many men. Take them down to the water, and I will sift them out for you there.

DELIVERANCE FROM THE SIN OF GLUTTONY

If I say, 'This one shall go with you,' he shall go; but if I say, 'This one shall not go with you,' he shall not go.'

So Gideon took the men down to the water. There the LORD told him, "Separate those who lap the water with their tongues like a dog from those who kneel down to drink." Three hundred men lapped with their hands to their mouths. All the rest got down on their knees to drink.

The LORD said to Gideon, "With the three hundred men that lapped I will save you and give the Midianites into your hands. Let all the other men go, each to his place." So Gideon sent the rest of the Israelites to their tents but kept the three hundred, who took over the provisions and trumpets of the others.

Now the camp of Midian lay below him in the valley. During that night the Lord said to Gideon, "Get up, go down against the camp, because I am going to give it into your hands. If you are afraid to attack, go down to the camp with your servant Purah and listen to what they are saying. Afterwards, you will be encouraged to attack the camp." So he and Purah his servant went to the outposts of the camp. The Midianites, the Amalekites and all the other eastern peoples had settled in the valley, thick as locusts. Their camels could no more be counted than the sand of the seashore.

Gideon arrived just as a man was telling a friend his dream. "I had a dream," he was saying. "A round loaf of barley bread came tumbling into the Midianite camp. It struck the tent with such force that the tent overturned and collapsed." His friend responded, "This can be nothing other than the sword of Gideon son of Joash, the Israelite. God has given the Midianites and the whole camp into his hands."

When Gideon heard the dream and its interpretation, he worshiped God. He returned to the camp of Israel and called out,

*"Get up! The LORD has given the Midianite camp into your hands."
Dividing the three hundred men into three companies, he placed
trumpets and empty jars in the hands of all of them, with torches
inside.*

*"Watch me," he told them. "Follow my lead. When I get to the
edge of the camp, do exactly as I do. When I and all who are with
me blow our trumpets, then from all around the camp blow yours and
shout, 'for the LORD and for Gideon.'"*

*Gideon and the three hundred men with him reached the edge
of the camp at the beginning of the middle watch, just after they
had changed the guard. They blew their trumpets and broke the jars
that were in their hands. The three companies blew the trumpets and
smashed the jars. Grasping the torches in their left hands and holding
in their right hands the trumpets they were to blow, they shouted,
"A sword for the LORD and for Gideon!" While each man held his
position around the camp, all the Midianites ran crying out as they
fled.*

*When the three hundred trumpets sounded, the LORD caused
the men throughout the camp to turn on each other with their swords.
The army fled to Beth Shittah towards Zererah as far as the border of
Abel Meholah near Tabbath. Israelites from Naphtali, Asher and all
Manaseh were called out, and they pursued the Midianites. Gideon
sent messengers throughout the hill country of Ephraim, saying,
"Come down against the Midianites and seize the waters of the Jordan
ahead of them as far as Beth Barah."*

*So all the men of Ephraim were called out and they took the
waters of the Jordan as far as Beth Barah. They also captured two of
the Midianite leaders, Oreb and Zeeb. They killed Oreb at the rock of
Oreb, and Zeeb at the winepress of Zeeb. They pursued the Midianites*

*and brought the heads of Oreb and Zeeb to Gideon, who was by the
Jordan* (Judges 7:1-25).

It was no small matter that 22,000 men withdrew from the
army because of fear!

God still found the 10.000 who were left not qualified to battle
for Him. He said to Gideon, "Take them down to the water, and I
will sift them out for you there."

At the water, some lapped the water with their tongues like
a dog. These could so drink water while carrying their military
equipment, food and all. Others knelt down to drink. Because they
had to get on their knees to drink, they necessarily had to put down
their equipment before kneeling.

Those who lapped were qualified for war. They were drinking
water in order to do the duty of life. Those who knelt down were
making it the duty of life to drink and so they were disqualified.

The attitude of those people to water exposed their hearts.
Some were ease-loving, indulgent and self-sparing. Others were
prepared for the harsh demands of war that made food a means to
an end and not an end in itself.

Those who are caught up with God's call on their lives and the
grave responsibilities to ensure that the lost hear the Gospel of Jesus
and turn to Him and be built into an army for the Lord give very
little attention to food. They are content with what God provides
while their hearts, heads and all are given to their goal.

Those who have no heavenly vision, and are pre-occupied with
no eternal issues, are pre-occupied with themselves, and give
endless attention to their food. Is it surprising that they go
nowhere? Is it surprising that they cannot be sent on God's errands.

Little things matter to God. They expose what is hidden in the
heart.

Does your attitude to who cooks your food,
what is cooked,
when it is cooked,
how it is cooked,
how much salt it contains,
how much meat it contains,
what type of meat it contains,
when the meat was bought,
where it was bought,
what ingredients were put in,
what temperature the food is,
what quantify was served,
when the same type of food was served previously,
what plate it was put in,
what cutlery were set with the food,
the type of glass for the water,
the amount of the water served,
the source of the water served,
and so on

say that you are a soldier or that you have been pushed aside as being too indulgent to fight God's battle?

If you have been laid aside because of indulgence with food,
time,
money,
energy,
and so on,

you should repent and seek the Lord. He will have mercy on you, transform you and enrol you once more into His army.

Amen.

The Desecration Of Samson The Nazirite

a. The Demands for a Nazirite

THE LORD SAID TO MOSES, *"Speak to the Israelites and say to them: If a man or woman wants to make a special vow, a vow of separation to the LORD as a Nazirite, he must abstain from wine and other fermented drink and must not drink vinegar made from wine or from other fermented drink. He must not drink grape juice or eat grapes or raisins. As long as he is a Nazirite, he must not eat anything that comes from the grapevine, not even the seeds or skins.*

"During the entire period of his vow of separation no razor may be used on his head. He must be holy until the period of his separation to the LORD is over; he must let the hair grow long. Throughout the period of his separation to the LORD he must not go near a dead body. Even if his own father or mother or brother or sister dies, he must not make himself ceremonially unclean on account of them, because the symbol of his separation to God is on his head. Throughout the period of his separation he is consecrated to the LORD.

"If someone dies suddenly in his presence, thus defiling the hair he has dedicated, he must shave his head on the day of his cleansing – the seventh day. Then on the eighth day he must bring two doves or two young pigeons to the priest at the entrance to the Tent of Meeting. The priest is to offer one as a sin offering and the other as a burnt offering to make atonement for him because he sinned by being in the presence of the dead body. That same day he is to consecrate his body. That same day he is to consecrate his head. He must dedicate himself to the LORD for the period of his separation and must bring a year-old male lamb as a guilt offering. The previous days do not count, because he became defiled during his separation.

"Now this is the law for the Nazirite when the period of his separation is over. He is to be brought to the entrance to the Tent of Meeting. There he is to present his offerings to the LORD: a year-old male lamb without defect for a burnt offering, a year-old ewe lamb without defect for a sin offering, a ram without defect for a fellowship offering together with their grain offerings and drink offerings, and a basket of bread made without yeast – cakes made of fine flour mixed with oil, and wafers spread with oil.

"'The priest is to present them, before the LORD and make the sin offering and the burnt offering. He is to present the basket of unleavened bread and is to sacrifice the ram as a fellowship offering to the LORD, together with its grain offering and drink offering.

"Then at the entrance to the Tent of Meeting, the Nazirite must shave off the hair that he dedicated. He is to take the hair and put it in the fire that is under the sacrifice of the fellowship offering.

"After the Nazirite has shaved off the hair of his dedication, the priest is to place in his hands a boiled shoulder of the ram, and a cake and a wafer from the basket, both made without yeast. The priest shall then wave them before the LORD as a wave offering; they are holy and belong to the priest, together with the breast that was waved and the thigh that was presented. After that, the Nazirite may drink wine.

'This is the law of the Nazirite who vows his offerings to the LORD in accordance with his separation in addition to whatever else he can afford. He must fulfil the vow he has made according to the law of the Nazirite' (Numbers 6 1- 21).

One of the demands for a Nazarite was that he should not be in the presence of a dead body. He was not to go near a dead body. Even if his father, mother, brother or sister were to die, he was to keep away from the dead body, because the symbol of his separation onto God is on his head. This was an unchanging law!

DELIVERANCE FROM THE SIN OF GLUTTONY

b. Samson A Nazarite

Again the Israelites did evil in the eyes of the LORD, so the LORD delivered them into the hands of the Philistines for forty years.

A certain man of Zorah, named Manoah, from the clan of the Danites, had a wife who was sterile and remained childless. The angel of the LORD appeared to her and said, "You are sterile and childless, but you are going to conceive and have a son. Now see to it that you drink no wine or other fermented drink and that you do not eat anything unclean, because you will conceive and give birth to a son. No razor may be used on his head, because the boy is to be a Nazirite, set apart to God from birth, and he will begin the deliverance of Israel from the hands of the Philistines."

Then the woman went to her husband and told him, "A man of God came to me. He looked like an angel of God, very awesome. I didn't ask him where he came from, and he didn't tell me his name. But he said to me 'You will conceive and give birth to a son. Now then, drink no wine or other fermented drink and do not eat anything unclean, because the boy will be a Nazirite of God from birth until the day of his death.'

Then Manoah prayed to the Lord, "O LORD, I beg you, let the man of God you sent to us come again to teach us how to bring up the boy who is to be born."

God heard Manoah, and the angel of God came again to the woman while she was out in the field; but her husband Manoah was not with her. The woman hurried to tell her husband, "He's here! The man who appeared to me the other day!"

Manoah got up and followed his wife. When he came to the man, he said, "Are you the one who talked to my wife?"

"I am," he said.

So Manoah asked him, "When your words are fulfilled, what is to be the rule for the boy's life and work?"

The angel of the LORD answered, "Your wife must do all that I have told her. She must not eat anything that comes from the grapevine, nor drink any wine or other fermented drink nor eat anything unclean. She must do everything I have commanded her."

Manoah said to the angel of the LORD, "We would like you to stay until we prepare a young goat for you" (Judges13: 1-15).

Samson's parents were told, "The boy will be a Nazirite of God from birth until the day of his death."

Samson was obviously told, "You are a Nazirite of God from birth until the day of your death?"

He was obviously told, "You are not to go near a dead body all the days of your life because you are a Nazirite of God."

Samson knew what the implications of his being a Nazirite were. He saw his hair and all the other things that put him aside. He also knew that he was not to go near the dead.

c. The Desecration and the Pathway to Freedom

Samson went down to Timnah and saw there a young Philistine woman. When he returned, he said to his father and mother, "I have seen a Philistine woman in Timna; now get her for me as my wife."

His father and mother replied, "Isn't there an acceptable woman among your relatives or among all our people? Must you go to the uncircumcised Philistines to get a wife?"

But Samson said to his father, "Get her for me. She's the right one for me." (His parents did not know that this was from the Lord, who was seeking an occasion to confront the Philistines; for at that time they were ruling over Israel.) Samson went down to Timnah together with his father and mother. As they approached the vineyards of Timnah, suddenly a young lion came roaring toward him. The

Spirit of the Lord came upon him in power so that he tore the lion apart with his bare hands as he might have torn a young goat. But he told neither his father nor his mother what he had done.

Then he went down and talked with the woman, and he liked her.

Sometime later he went back to marry her, he turned aside to look at the lion's carcass. In it was a swarm of bees and some honey, which he scooped out with his hands and ate as he went along. When he rejoined his parents, he gave them some, and they too ate it. But he did not tell them that he had taken the honey from the lion's carcass.

Now his father went down to see the woman. And Samson made a feast there, as was customary for bridegrooms (Judges 14:1-10).

Samson was a Nazirite!

When the Spirit of God came upon him, he became another man. In the situation at hand, when the Spirit of the Lord came upon him in power, he tore the lion that came roaring towards him with his bare hands as he might have torn a young goat. The Lord saved his life and that was great.

According to God's purposes for Samson's life, that was the end of the incident because Samson, a Nazirite, was not to go near a dead body. However, Samson thought differently. For him, being a Nazirite meant spiritual power but it did not mean denying himself anything. He went to look at the dead body of the lion. In it was a swarm of bees and some honey. He might have hesitated because he could not take the honey without touching the carcass. Then he threw all away, touched the carcass and removed some of the honey which he ate and gave some to his parents. He desecrated himself because of the desire to eat the honey.

Samson was not dying of starvation when he saw the honey. He could have continued his journey without eating anything had the honey not been there. He just decided that the laws of God could be disobeyed with impunity and he decided not to reflect on the consequence.

It did not end with Samson touching the dead lion. Because of the honey, he came up with a riddle which the Philistines could not explain. He went and slew thirty men of Ashkelon, stripped them of their belongings and gave their clothes to those who had explained the riddle. To strip them of their belongings, Samson came into further contact with the dead, a thing that was forbidden for him who was a Nazirite. He had thus started with the love of food and then continued with the love of fame as he told them the riddle. He refused to take his consecration seriously.

Samson thus set things rolling along a path in which he denied himself nothing. He acted like the king who was later to express his lifestyle as follows, "I denied myself nothing my eyes desired, I refused my heart no pleasure." (Ecclesiastes 2:10).

The pathway that Samson chose led to the release of the secret of his strength, the loss of the locks on his head, the loss of his power, the loss of his eyes and a life of humiliation as an entertainer of his enemies!

What a sad end!

It must be remembered that that road was entered into when he refused to say, "NO!" to a desire to eat honey from a forbidden source.

Remember that each indulgent act contributes to making you into an indulgent person and the end may be sad, very sad.

When your appetites tell you to take a second helping of some food,

slice of some cake,

piece of some meat,

spoonful,

it is an invitation to build a self-gratifying character. That character is built a little at a time until the power to be able to say, "No," to food is lost completely.

Are you at the beginning of that pathway? Won't you call upon the Lord to help you break free today?

Are you already advanced along that pathway? The Holy Spirit is willing to come to your aid. You may not be able to help yourself. He is able to help you.

Are you already established as a slave to food and all attempts to break lose have failed and failed again? May be you tried to break free with the power of your will and your will failed you. You tried to break free on the basis of the knowledge you have and your knowledge failed you. You called your strong feelings to work but they too failed. You have tried one programme made by man after another. Each seemed to have worked with others, but none would work in your case.

We bring you a word of hope. Your love for or slavery to food is a work of the flesh. The methods that you have tried have been methods of the flesh. The flesh cannot deliver you from the power of the flesh. Instead of turning to your will, mind and emotions for help, turn to the Holy Spirit. He has been dwelling in you since you let Jesus come into your life. He is there. Tell Him that you are in trouble. Tell Him you are not able to break loose from the habit that has imprisoned you. Tell Him you believe that He can help you. Ask Him to help you. After you have asked Him to help you, wait in silence before Him. Wait until He speaks to you. He will speak to you. Obey what He says. After you have obeyed Him, report back to Him. He will tell you what to do next. Obey. Walk with Him along these lines and you will soon find that you have been delivered.

The wonder about the Holy Spirit as the Deliverer is that He tells you what to do and gives you Himself as the power with which to obey. He cannot fail. He is most able.

Amen.

The Gluttony Of The Priests Hophni And Phinehas

A. Gluttony committed

ELI'S SONS WERE WICKED men; they had no regard for the LORD. Now it was the practice of the priests with the people that whenever anyone offered a sacrifice and while the meat was being boiled, the servant of the priest would come with a three-pronged fork in his hand. He would plunge it into the pan or kettle or cauldron or pot, and the priest would take for himself whatever the fork brought up. This is how they treated all the Israelites who came to Shiloh. But even before the fat was burned, the servant of the priest would come and say to the man who was sacrificing, "Give the priest some meat to roast; he won't accept boiled meat from you, but only raw."

If the man said to him, "Let the fat be burned up first, and then take whatever you want," the servant would then answer, "No, hand it over now; if you don't I'll take it by force."

This sin of the young men was very great in the LORD's sight, for they were treating the LORD's offering with contempt (1 Samuel 2:12-17).

Eli's sons were wicked. They had no regard for the Lord. They greedily interfered with the sacrifices that were being offered to the Lord. They had regard only for their stomachs. They wanted meat and meat and they wanted it in a hurry. They knew that the fat belonged to the Lord exclusively. They also knew that after the fat was burned up, they could have what they wanted. However, they would not wait. They threatened the people and took away what they wanted and when they wanted. It ought to have been: "The Lord first." Rather, they established another maxim, "Hophni and Phinehas first." They overthrew the Lord and enthroned themselves.

Gluttony is overthrowing the Lord and enthroning self!

Gluttony is saying "No" to self-denial and "Yes" to self-gratification!

The sin of the priests was very great in the Lord's sight, for they were treating the Lord's offering with contempt!

B. Warning

Now a man of God came to Eli and said to him, "This is what the LORD says; 'Did I not clearly reveal myself to your father's house when they were in Egypt under Pharaoh? I chose your father out of all the tribes of Israel to be my priest, to go up to my altar, to burn incense, and to wear an ephod in my presence. I also gave your father's house all the offerings made with fire by the Israelites. Why do you scorn my sacrifice and offering that I prescribed for my dwelling? Why do you honour your sons more than me by fattening yourselves on the choice parts of every offering made by my people Israel?

Therefore the LORD, the God of Israel, declares; 'I promised that your house and your father's house would minister before me forever.' But now the LORD declares; 'Far be it from me! Those who honour me I will honour, but those who despise me will be disdained. The time is coming when I will cut short your strength and the strength of your father's house, so that there will not be an old man in your family line and you will see distress in my dwelling. Although good will be done to Israel, in your family line there will never be an old man. Every one of you that I do not cut off from my altar will be spared only to blind your eyes with tears and to grieve your heart, and all your descendants will die in the prime of life.

'And what happens to your two sons, Hophni and Phinehas, will be a sign to you - they will both die on the same day. I will raise up for myself a faithful priest, who will do according to what is in my heart and mind. I will firmly establish his house, and he will minister before my anointed one always. Then everyone left in your family line will come and bow down before him for a piece of silver and a crust of bread and plead, "Appoint me to some priestly office so that I can have food to eat"' (1 Samuel 2: 27-36).

The warning came to Eli and consequently to his sons. God promised to punish them and the whole family line for many years to come!

What was their sin? It was clearly stated, "Fattening yourselves on the choice parts of every offering made by my people Israel."

Have you thought about how fat you are? Do you know how many extra kilograms of weight you have been carrying? You have been fattening yourself! You have been fattening yourself! You have been fattening yourself!

In India, 25,000 people pass into eternity daily who have never heard the Gospel of Jesus Christ. Part of the reason why they are perishing is the fact that you have been fattening yourself with excess food while they have been starving of the Gospel unto a Christless grave! Have you thought of how many people would have been reached with the Gospel had you not buried the money that would have been used for their evangelization in fattening yourself? Will you not repent and do something about it today?

The sons of Eli were warned, but they did not heed the warning. Has the Lord not warned you about your gluttony and the consequences thereof?

DELIVERANCE FROM THE SIN OF GLUTTONY

How many times has He warned you?

Do you know how many people have been denied the Gospel because of your gluttony? You may be a fat or a thin glutton. However, beware! There are people who are being denied the Lord because of your attitude to food. You may not have been told but the facts are there. There are people who are waiting to see you delivered from the power of food in order to turn themselves over to the Lord Jesus about whom you are talking. They are saying to themselves; "If that Jesus cannot deliver this one from the power of food, how can I go to Him for deliverance from

1. Pride
2. Adultery
3. Fornication
4. Lying
5. Drunkenness
6. Hypocrisy
7. Bitterness
8. and so on.

How can you who are chained by gluttony proclaim the message of freedom to another who like you, is bound by another vice?

The Bible says, *The acts of the sinful nature are obvious: sexual immorality, impurity, debauchery, idolatry and witchcraft; hatred, discord, jealousy, fits of rage, selfish ambition, dissensions, factions and envy; drunkenness, orgies (gluttony), and the like. I warn you, as I did before, that those who live like this will not inherit the Kingdom of God* (Galatians 5: 19-21).

Is the glutton better before God than the one who practices the following:

1. Sexual immorality,
2. Idolatry,
3. Theft,
4. Witchcraft,
5. Envy

Does the Lord not frown at all of them?

Does the Lord not warn all and call all to depart from all of them?

Has he not warned you personally?

God warned the children of Eli. He told them, "I will raise up for myself a faithful priest who will do according to what is in my heart and mind." The Lord was saying to the sons of Eli, "You could repent and become faithful priests who do what is in My heart and mind."

They thus received God's offer but threw it away. Meat meant more to them than anything else. The fleeting pleasures of meat in their mouths meant more to them than the permanent blessings of God.

They were warned that the judgment would affect their offspring for years to come, but they were not moved.

Have you thought about what your gluttony may mean to your offspring? They could become gluttons. That is bad enough. Worst still, they could also become liars, thieves, prostitutes, nonentities, homosexuals, and practice every evil. The sin of gluttony harboured in you for years may open a door for countless disasters in their lives. You have been warned. Do something about it. Do it today. Do it now.

C. The Judgment

Now the Israelites went out to fight against the Philistines. The Israelites camped at Ebenezer, and the Philistines at Aphek. The Philistines deployed their forces to meet Israel, and as the battle spread, Israel was defeated by the Philistines, who killed about four thousand of them on the battlefield.

When the soldiers returned to camp, the elders of Israel asked, "Why did the LORD bring defeat upon us today before the Philistines? Let us bring the ark of the LORD's covenant from Shiloh, so that it may go with us and save us from the hand of our enemies."

So the people sent men to Shiloh, and they brought back the ark of the covenant of the LORD Almighty, who is enthroned between the cherubim. And Eli's two sons, Hophni and Phinehas, were there with the ark of the covenant of God.

When the ark of the LORD's covenant came into the camp, all Israel raised such a great shout that the ground shook. Hearing the uproar, the Philistines asked, "What's all this shouting in the Hebrew camp?"

When they learned that the ark of the LORD had come into the camp, the Philistines were afraid. "A god has come into the camp," they said. "We're in trouble! Nothing like this has happened before. Woe to us! Who will deliver us from the hand of these mighty gods? They are the gods who struck the Egyptians with all kinds of plagues in the desert. Be strong, Philistines! Be men, or you will be subjected to the Hebrews, as they have been to you. Be men, and fight!"

So the Philistines fought, and the Israelites were defeated and every man fled to his tent. The slaughter was very great; Israel lost thirty thousand foot soldiers. The ark of God was captured, and Eli's two sons, Hophni and Phinehas, died (1Samuel 4:1-11).

Hophni and Phinehas did not heed God's warning. They continued in their gluttony and added sexual immorality to it. Then the Lord did what He promised. They were killed in one day. They did not die alone. Their father died on the same day.

The wife of Phinehas died on the same day.

30.000 Israelit soldiers died on the same day.

The ark of the Lord was captured.

God had kept His Word. God always keeps His Word.

What about God's Word that their sin would affect their offspring for many years to come? Samuel became leader after the sons of Eli had been killed. After Samuel, Saul became leader. After Saul, David became leader and David was succeeded by Solomon. During Solomon's reign the offspring of Eli was still suffering partly because of the sin of Hophni and Phinehas. The Bible says, *To Abiathar the priest the king said, "Go back to your fields in Anathoth. You deserve to die, but I will not put you to death now, because you carried the ark of the Sovereign Lord before my father David and shared all my father's hardships." So Solomon removed Abiathar from the priesthood of the Lord, fulfilling the word the Lord had spoken at Shiloh about the house of Eli* (1Kings 2: 26-27).

A Word to Spiritual Leaders

All over the world there are pastors, evangelists, bible teachers, missionary leaders and various workers for the Lord who are overweight. Many are as if they were pregnant. They do not commit adultery. They do not drink alcohol. They condemn these works of the flesh in strong language. I congratulate them on this.

DELIVERANCE FROM THE SIN OF GLUTTONY

My only problem is that while the adulterer is drunk with women and the alcoholic is drunk with alcohol, they are drunk with food.

If God is just and fair, then such preachers will receive from the Lord what He will give to their kind who practice adultery, drunkenness and the like.

God is not mocked! If some people choose some works of the flesh as objects for severe attack while wallowing in others, we can be sure that God will not close His eyes to their sins.

If you are overweight, you are denying the Lord by your gluttony and your sin will catch up with you.

This is the day on which you should call your sin by name and repent of it and abandon it completely. The Holy Spirit is near and will help you.

Ask Him to help you now!

The Seduction Of The Man Of God From Judah

*BY THE WORD OF THE LORD a man of God came from Judah
to Bethel, as Jeroboam was standing by the altar to make an offering.
He cried out against the altar by the word of the LORD: "O altar,
altar! This is what the LORD says: 'A son named Josiah will be born
to the house of David. On you he will sacrifice the priests of the high
places who now make offerings here, and human bones will be burned
on you.' That same day the man of God gave a sign: "This is the sign
the LORD has declared: The altar will be split apart and the ashes on
it will be poured out."*

*When King Jeroboam heard what the man of God cried out
against the altar at Bethel, he stretched out his hand from the altar
and said, "Seize him!" But the hand he stretched out towards the man
shrivelled up, so that he could not pull it back. Also, the altar was split
apart and its ashes poured out according to the sign given by the man
of God by the word of the LORD.*

*Then the king said to the man of God, "Intercede with the LORD
your God and pray for me that my hand may be restored." So the man
of God interceded with the LORD, and the king's hand was restored
and became as it was before.*

*The king said to the man of God, "Come home with me and have
something to eat, and I will give you a gift."*

*But the man of God answered the king, "Even if you were to give
me half your possessions, I would not go with you, nor would I eat
bread or drink water here. For I was commanded by the word of the
LORD: 'You must not eat bread or drink water or return by the way*

you came.' So he took another road and did not return by the way he had come to Bethel.

Now there was a certain old prophet living in Bethel, whose sons came and told him all that the man of God had done there that day. They also told their father what he had said to the king. Their father asked them, "Which way did he go?" And his sons showed him which road the man of God from Judah had taken. So he said to his sons, "Saddle the donkey for me." And when they had saddled the donkey for him, he mounted it and rode after the man of God. He found him sitting under an oak tree and asked, "Are you the man of God who came from Judah?" "I am," he replied.

So the prophet said to him, "Come home with me and eat."

The man of God said, "I cannot turn back and go with you, nor can I eat bread or drink water with you in this place. I have been told by the word of the LORD: 'You must not eat bread or drink water there or return by the way you came.'"

The old prophet answered, "I too am a prophet, as you are. And an angel said to me by the word of the LORD: 'Bring him back with you to your house so that he may eat bread and drink water.'" (But he was lying to him.) So the man of God returned with him and ate and drank in his house.

While they were sitting at the table, the word of the LORD came to the old prophet who had brought him back. He cried out to the man of God who had come from Judah, "This is what the LORD says: 'You have defied the word of the LORD and have not kept the command the LORD your God gave you. You came back and ate bread and drank water in the place where he told you not to eat or drink. Therefore your body will not be buried in the tomb of your fathers.'

When the man of God had finished eating and drinking, the prophet who had brought him back saddled his donkey for him. As he went on his way, a lion met him on the road and killed him, and his body was thrown down on the road, with both the donkey and the lion standing beside it. Some people who passed by saw the body thrown down there, with the lion standing beside the body, and they went and reported it in the city where the old prophet lived.

When the prophet who had brought him back from his journey heard of it, he said, "It is the man of God who defied the word of the LORD. The LORD has given him over to the lion, which has mauled him and killed him, as the word of the LORD had warned him."

The prophet said to his sons, "Saddle the donkey for me," and they did so. Then he went out and found the body thrown down on the road with the donkey and the lion standing beside it. The lion had neither eaten the body nor mauled the donkey. So the prophet picked up the body of the man of God, laid it on the donkey, and brought it back to his own city to mourn for him and bury him. Then he laid the body in his own tomb, and they mourned over him and said, "Oh my brother!"

After burying him, he said to his sons, "When I die, bury me in the grave where the man of God is buried; lay my bones besides his bones. For the message he declared by the word of the LORD against the altar in Bethel and against all the shrines on the high places in the towns of Samaria will certainly come true" (1 Kings 13: 1-32).

This man of God was in many ways outstanding. He came to Bethel from Judah by the word of the Lord. He cried out against the altar as Jeroboam was standing by it to make an offering, without fearing the king. When the King tried to seize him, the hand he stretched out towards the man shrivelled up, so that he could not pull it back. The altar on which Jeroboam wanted to sacrifice split apart and its ashes poured out as the man of God had said. At the king's request the man of God interceded with the Lord and the king's hand that had shrivelled was restored. He rejected an offer of food and a gift by the king. He was truly outstanding. How few there are like him in our day! O, how few men of God there are on the scene in our day! Lord God Almighty, won't you raise up some? We plead, dear Lord, that You should stretch out Your mighty hand and give us men of God. This need is great, O God!

The man unfortunately failed when it came to saying, "No" to food. The Lord had commanded him, "You must not eat bread or drink water or return by the way you came."

The man of God was very sure of this. He said to the king, "Even if you were to give me half your possessions, I would not go with you, nor would I eat bread or drink water here. For I was commanded by the word of the Lord: "You must not eat bread or drink water or return by the way you came." He also refused to listen to the king. He was obedient.

When he faced the prophet, the instructions to him were still very clear and he stated them clearly – no bread, no water, no returning by the same route.

Then he faltered. There must have been something in his heart that opened up to food. The Bible says, *Each one is tempted when, by his own evil desire, he is dragged away and enticed. Then after desire has conceived, it gives birth to sin, and sin, when it is full-grown, gives birth to death* (James 1:14-15).

We can set this out as follows: Desire Enticement Sin Death

There was desire in the heart of the man of God for food and drink. He did not deal with the desire. He ought to have gotten rid of the desire, but he allowed it there and nourished it. He let it grow. The old prophet brought the false prophecy to him when the desire for food and drink was fully grown in his heart. Consequently, the offer of food enticed him. Because he was enticed, he did not ask how the prophecy from the old prophet could be contradicting the initial prophecy which he had received. He was sure of the initial prophecy since parts of it had already been fulfilled. That which contradicted a part of the first prophecy was most-likely to be false. However, he desired food and the "prophecy" helped him to be enticed. He then went and ate, thus committing sin and soon afterwards he was a dead man.

The death sentence came in the following words, "You have defied the word of the Lord and you have not kept the command the Lord your God gave you. You came back and ate bread and drank water in the place where he told you not to eat or drink. Therefore your body will not be buried in the tomb of your fathers."

The man of God was disobedient. However, the lion was not disobedient.

Responsibility and Judgment

Some may ask if the man of God from Judah was not treated too harshly by the Lord. He was certainly not treated too harshly. He had heard God's voice from the beginning. He wielded mighty power. God backed his every word. God moved in and caused the hand that attempted to lay hold of him to shrivel up. His intercession was instantly heard. God had invested so much into him. He operated at a plane of power and might that few know anything about. For such privileges God demands perfect obedience and total separation from every lust of the flesh. The man of God had spiritual power and entertained love for food together in the same being. God punished him to show His outright disapproval of mixtures.

Spiritual responsibilities go along with judgment. The greater the man, the greater his responsibilities. The greater his responsibilities, the greater the power that he wields. The greater the power that he wields, the greater the judgment that would fall upon him for disobedience.

Moses exercised enormous power. However, when he disobeyed the Lord once, he was disqualified from leadership and sent away to die prematurely on the mountain.

God demands perfection from those who would wield spiritual power in His name. Anyone who desires to serve the Lord must seek and know the power of God. He must also seek and render to God total obedience in everything. If the Lord allows His power to become operational in a life, that person must receive it as a special call to radical renunciation of every indulgence of the flesh and a call to radical consecration to the Lord. If these two are lacking or if anyone of them is lacking or is not present in full measure, he will find that he has worked himself to a place of ruin.

The man of God from Judah desired food and was enticed by it. What do you desire? Is it money, women or fame?

If it is any of these, get rid of it at once before the desire entices you to sin and death. The sooner you act, the better for you. God is waiting for you now. Turn to Him now and ask Him to take away the desire for fortune, females or fame that you may have. Ask Him to replace it with a desire to know and love the Lord Jesus increasingly and to bring all men to Him. Let this new desire possess you and you will not only be safe but you will flourish spiritually and in all other ways.

Glory be to God!
Amen.

The Gluttony Of The Corinthians

IN THE FOLLOWING DIRECTIVES I have no praise for you, for your meetings do more harm than good. In the first place, I hear that when you come together as a church, there are divisions among you, and to some extent I believe it. No doubt there have to be differences among you to show which of you have God's approval. When you come together, it is not the Lord's Supper you eat, for as you eat, each of you goes ahead without waiting for anybody else. One remains hungry, another gets drunk. Don't you have homes to eat and drink in? Or do you despise the church of God and humiliate those who have nothing? What shall I say to you? Shall I praise you for this? Certainly not!

For I received from the Lord what I also passed on to you. The Lord Jesus, on the night he was betrayed, took bread, and when he had given thanks, he broke it and said, "This is my body, which is for you; do this in remembrance of me." In the same way, after supper he took the cup, saying, "This cup is the new covenant in my blood; do this, whenever you drink it, in remembrance of me." For whenever you eat this bread and drink this cup, you proclaim the Lord's death until he comes.

Therefore, whoever eats the bread or drinks the cup of the Lord in an unworthy manner will be guilty of sinning against the body and blood of the Lord. A man ought to examine himself before he eats of the bread and drinks of the cup. For anyone who eats and drinks without recognizing the body of the Lord eats and drinks judgment on himself. That is why many among you are weak and sick, and a number of you have fallen asleep. But if we judged ourselves, we would not come under judgment. When we are judged by the Lord, we are being disciplined so that we will not be condemned with the world.

So then, my brothers, when you come together to eat, wait for each other. If anyone is hungry, he should eat at home, so that when you meet together it may not result in judgment.

And when I come I will give further directions (I Corinthians 11:17-34).

When the Corinthians met for the Lord's Supper, gluttony was committed. Some had nothing to eat whereas others had more than enough. Some had nothing to drink while others were drunk.

Because of this sin of gluttony and drunkenness, judgment came upon them and they received judgment in proportion to their sin. Some were weak. Others were sick; while others died. These three conditions were brought upon them by the sin of gluttony. We can set it out as follows:

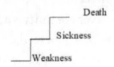

Death
Sickness
Weakness

Why should it not be the case that there are believers today who are weak in their bodies because of gluttony? Why should it not be considered as a possibility that there are believers who are sick today because of gluttony? Why should it not be confessed today that some believers have died because of gluttony? Is it not fair to present it as follows:

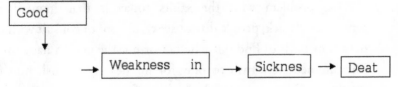

Good → Weakness in → Sicknes → Deat

Glutto

WE KNOW OF BELIEVERS who were healed of diseases when they came to the Lord Jesus or who received an overall improvement in their health condition after conversion.

We also know of the same believers becoming weaker in body and then sick in body and some have actually died. Might this not be the salary they earned for gluttony or some other work of the flesh like sexual immorality, impurity, debauchery, idolatry, witchcraft, hatred, discord, jealousy, fits of rage, selfish ambition, dissensions, factions, envy, or drunkenness and the like?

It is most likely.

Every sin that a believer commits is like a knife with which the heart of God is being pierced!

Every sin that a believer commits is a knife with which his own spirit, soul and body are being pierced.

No one is quite the same after he has sinned, regardless of whether the sin was lying, anger, jealousy, pride or gluttony. A fatal blow is plunged into his physical and spiritual health. His spirit is affected; his mind, will and emotions are affected. His muscles, blood and bones are affected.

The works of the flesh, all works of the flesh are great enemies. They must be treated as such.

The problem with the saints today is that immediately someone falls sick, people do not seek the Lord or consult with the person or both to find out whether or not the person has sinned. They immediately rush to pray for his healing or rush him for treatment. Can prayers for the healing of a disease that has resulted from the sin of gluttony or any other sin be heard before the sinner has acknowledged his sin, confessed it to the Lord, forsaken it and been forgiven? I leave it for your prayerful meditation.

Amen.

The Teaching Of The Lord Jesus On Food And Feeding

Do Not Worry!

Therefore I tell you, do not worry about your life, what you will eat or drink; or about your body, what you will wear. Is not life more important than clothes? Look at the birds of the air; they do not sow or reap or store away in barns, and yet your heavenly Father feeds them. Are you not much more valuable than they? Who of you by worrying can add a single hour to his life?

And why do you worry about clothes? See how the lilies of the field grow. They do not labour or spin. Yet I tell you that not even Solomon in all his splendour was dressed like one of these. If that is how God clothes the grass of the field, which is here today and tomorrow is thrown into the fire, will he not much more clothe you, O you of little faith? So do not worry, saying, "What shall we eat?" or 'What shall we drink?' or 'What shall we wear?' For the pagans run after all these things, and your heavenly Father knows that you need them. But seek first his kingdom and his righteousness, and all these things will be given to you as well.

Therefore do not worry about tomorrow, for tomorrow will worry about itself. Each day has enough trouble of its own (Matthew 6:25-34).

The Lord Jesus taught that those who are His should not worry about what they would eat because their heavenly Father would feed them.

He was not calling His own to irresponsibility and laziness. Rather, He was calling them to labour from a position of rest. He was calling them to labour with God as their provider.

If you do not have what to eat, if you have too much to eat; if you are a glutton who is thin, if you are a glutton who is overweight, God calls you first to His rest and then to His solution to your problem.

He calls you away from worry, for worry will not solve your problem. It will add to your problem and may raise new problems for you.

Fasting

WHEN YOU FAST, DO NOT look sombre as the hypocrites do, for they disfigure their faces to show men they are fasting. I tell you the truth; they have received their reward in full. But when you fast, put oil on your head and wash your face, so that it will not be obvious to men that you are fasting but only to your Father, who is unseen; and your Father, who sees what is done in secret, will reward you (Matthew 6:16-18).

The Lord Jesus taught that those who are feeding in the will of God, will as a part of their feeding programme withdraw from food for hours, days or weeks to fast before returning to their normal eating programme.

The fast will accomplish spiritual goals and may also accomplish physical goals by granting the body organs that have to do with feeding much needed rest. Those gluttons whose gluttony is manifested in excess weight lose some of the extra weight and the entire body is moved to a plane of better health.

The fast helps all who are under the slavery of food to break lose for the duration of the fast. They can then begin to eat under the leadership of the Holy Spirit when the fast ends and in this way, have their problem solved once and for all.

Let Nothing Be Wasted - 1

SOME TIME AFTER THIS, Jesus crossed to the far shore of the Sea of Galilee (that is, the Sea of Tiberias), and a great crowd of people followed him because they saw the miraculous signs he had performed on the sick. Then Jesus went up on a mountainside and sat down with his disciples. The Jewish Passover Feast was near.

When Jesus looked up and saw a great crowd coming towards him, he said to Philip, "Where shall we buy bread for these people to eat?" He asked this only to test him, for he already had in mind what he was going to do.

Philip answered him, "Eight months' wages would not buy enough bread for each one to have a bite!"

Another of his disciples, Andrew, Simon Peter's brother, spoke up, "Here is a boy with five small barley loaves and two small fish, but how far will they go among so many?"

Jesus said, "Make the people sit down." There was plenty of grass in that place, and the men sat down, about five thousand of them. Jesus then took the loaves, gave thanks, and distributed to those who were seated as much as they wanted. He did the same with the fish.

DELIVERANCE FROM THE SIN OF GLUTTONY

When they had all had enough to eat, he said to his disciples, "Gather the pieces that are left over. Let nothing be wasted." So they gathered them and filled twelve baskets with the pieces of the five barley loaves left over by those who had eaten (John 6:1-13).

The Lord wants people fed.

He performed a miracle. With five barley loaves and two small fish, he fed a population that included five thousand men besides women and children. It was a far-reaching miracle.

The people ate as much as they wanted both of the loaves and of the fish.

There were leftovers. The Lord Jesus did not say, "Do not bother to gather the leftovers. I will perform another miracle when the need arises!"

He instead commanded, "Gather the pieces that are left over. Let nothing be wasted." That command was obeyed and the pieces of bread and fish that were left over filled twelve baskets.

The Lord Jesus said, "Let nothing be wasted." The Godhead is opposed to waste. Gluttony is a process of wasting. If a man's body needs one piece of meat and he eats two, he has wasted one. If it needs two oranges and he eats three, he has wasted one. If it needs one bowl of rice and he eats two, he has wasted one. If he needs one glass of coffee and he drinks three, he has wasted two.

Gluttony is eating what the body does not need to function at the optimum, at the best. Even if the body burns up all the excesses so that no extra weight is visible on the body, the person who eats what the body does not need or who eats more than the body needs has sinned before the Lord. He has disobeyed the command, "Let nothing be wasted."

Anyone who eats what he does not need is disobedient to the Lord.

Anyone who possesses more clothes than he needs is disobedient to the Lord.

Anyone who owns two cars when he really needs only one is disobedient to the Lord.

Anyone who owns anything that he does not need is disobedient to the Lord.

May the Lord help you to obey the command, "Let nothing be wasted," in your feeding life and in every other aspect of your life.

Praise the Lord!

Let Nothing Be Wasted - 2

JESUS LEFT THERE AND went along the Sea of Galilee. Then he went up on a mountainside and sat down. Great crowds came to him, bringing the lame, the blind, the crippled, the mute and many others, and laid them at his feet: and he healed them. The people were amazed when they saw the mute speaking, the crippled made well, the lame walking and the blind seeing. And they praised the God of Israel.

Jesus called his disciples to him and said, "I have compassion for these people; they have already been with me three days and have nothing to eat, I do not want to send them away hungry, or they may collapse on the way."

His disciples answered, "Where could we get enough bread in this remote place to feed such a crowd?"

"How many loaves do you have?" Jesus asked.

"Seven," they replied, "and a few small fish."

He told the crowd to sit down on the ground. Then he took the seven loaves and the fish, and when he had given thanks, he broke them and gave them to the disciples, and they in turn to the people. They all ate and were satisfied. Afterwards the disciples picked up seven basketfuls of broken pieces that were left over. The number of those who ate was four thousand, besides women and children (Matthew 15:29-38).

The Lord Jesus fed another crowd miraculously. This time there were seven loaves and a few small fish. The crowd was made up of four thousand men besides the women and the children.

Again the crowd ate and was satisfied.

There were leftovers.

The disciples had learnt the lesson. They did not wait for the Lord to tell them to pick up the remains. They had been told before, thus, and they remembered the message and obeyed it.

Oh, that we would receive the Lord's instructions and obey them! Oh, that we would learn each lesson the first time that he teaches us. Oh, that we would spare Him the waste of time that is involved in teaching one lesson over and over.

Did you learn the lesson: "Let nothing be wasted." Is that lesson already written in your life? Is it being lived out?

Blessed are you if the Lord will not have to teach you that lesson again and again.

Amen.

All Foods Are Clean!

THE PHARISEES AND SOME of the teachers of the law who had come from Jerusalem gathered round Jesus and saw some of his disciples eating food with hands that were "unclean", that is, unwashed. (The Pharisees and all the Jews do not eat unless they give their hands a ceremonial washing, holding to the tradition of the elders. When they come from the marketplace they do not eat unless they wash. And they observe many other traditions, such as the washing of cups, pitchers and kettles.)

So the Pharisees and teachers of the law asked Jesus, "Why don't your disciples live according to the tradition of the elders instead of eating their food with 'unclean' hands?"

He replied, "Isaiah was right when he prophesied about you hypocrites; as it is written:

"'These people honour me with their lips, but their hearts are far from me.

They worship me in vain: their teachings are but rules taught by men."

You have let go of the commands of God and are holding on to the traditions of men."

And he said to them: "You have a fine way of setting aside the commands of God in order to observe your own traditions! For Moses said, 'Honour your father and your mother,' and anyone who curses his father or mother must be put to death.' But you say that if a man says to his father or mother: "Whatever help you might otherwise have received from me is Corban' (that is, a gift devoted to God), then you no longer let him do anything for his father or mother. Thus you nullify the word of God by your tradition that you have handed down. And you do many things like that."

Again Jesus called the crowd to him and said, "Listen to me, everyone, and understand this. Nothing outside a man can make him 'unclean' by going into him. Rather, it is what comes out of a man that makes him 'unclean.'"

After he had left the crowd and entered the house, his disciples asked him about this parable. "Are you so dull?" he asked. "Don't you see that nothing that enters a man from the outside can make him 'unclean'? For it doesn't go into his heart but into his stomach and then out of his body." (In saying this, Jesus declared all foods "clean".)

He went on: "What comes out of a man is what makes him 'unclean'. For from within, out of men's hearts, come evil thoughts, sexual immorality, theft, murder, adultery, greed, malice, deceit, lewdness, envy, slander, arrogance and folly. All these evils come from inside and make a man 'unclean'" (Mark 7:1-23).

The Pharisees were given to rules and regulations about washing hands, eating and the rest. They observed many traditions and would have wanted Jesus and His disciples to observe them too. They were not caught up with the commandments of God. Rather, they were caught up with their own traditions. The Lord Jesus condemned this. He said that a person went wrong through what came out of his heart and not through what went into his stomach.

In the Mosaic law there were clean and unclean animals. The clean were to be eaten and the unclean not to be eaten. Jesus said, "Nothing that enters a man from outside can make a man "unclean" for it does not go into his heart but into his stomach and then out of his body." In saying this, Jesus declared all foods clean.

Halleluiah! Jesus has declared all foods clean. Jesus has declared all animals clean. All can now be eaten with thanksgiving to God. No one should then be praised or despised on the basis of the type of food he eats. All foods are clean. All are acceptable. All are made by God and given by God to be received with thanksgiving.

Glory be to the Lord!

Amen.

Eat Whatever They Give You

AFTER THIS THE LORD appointed seventy-two others and sent them two by two ahead of him to every town and place where he was about to go. He told them, "The harvest is plentiful, but the workers are few. Ask the Lord of the harvest, therefore, to send out workers into his harvest field. Go! I am sending you out like lambs among wolves. Do not take a purse or bag or sandals; and do not greet anyone on the road.

"When you enter a house, first say, 'Peace to this house.' If a man of peace is there, your peace will rest on him; if not, it will return to you. Stay in that house, eating and drinking whatever they give you, for the worker deserves his wages. Do not move around from house to house.

When you enter a town and are welcomed, eat what is set before you (Luke 10:1-8).

In sending the seventy-two out, He commanded them to "Eat whatever they give you."

How this command has been disobeyed! The missionaries want food sent to them from home. They are not eating whatever is given to them or available for them in their new "home land".

Africans transport African food to Europe!

Europeans transport European food to Africa!

Bread made in Douala is transported to Yaounde so that the brethren in Yaounde may eat Douala made bread. The brethren in Yaounde transport Yaounde-made bread to Douala so that the brethren in Douala may eat Yaounde-made bread!

This is part of the worship of food and the belly.

DELIVERANCE FROM THE SIN OF GLUTTONY

The Lord Jesus commanded, "Eat whatever they give you." He knew what He was saying. He was right. He is right. We disobey Him to our own peril.

Different localities have different foods available. Only the glutton with his gluttonous habits will find it difficult to fit into a new location with different foods and different feeding habits!

May God help us to obey! Amen.

The Example Of The Lord Jesus On Food And Feeding

Fasting

Jesus, full of the Holy Spirit, returned from the Jordan and was led by the Spirit in the desert, where for forty days he was tempted by the devil. He ate nothing during those days, and at the end of them he was hungry.

Then the devil said to him, "If you are the Son of God, tell this stone to become bread. Jesus answered, "It is written, 'Man does not live on bread alone.'"

The devil led him up to a high place and showed him in an instant all the kingdoms of the world. And he said to him, "I will give you all their authority and splendour, for it has been given to me, and I can give it to anyone I want to. So if you worship me, it will all be yours."

Jesus answered, "It is written: 'Worship the Lord your God and serve him only.'

The devil led him to Jerusalem and had him stand on the highest point of the temple. "If you are the Son of God," he said, "throw yourself down from here. For it is written: "'He will command his angels concerning you to guard you carefully; they will lift you up in their hands, so that you will not strike your foot against a stone.'"

Jesus answered, "It says: Do not put the Lord your God to the test.""

When the devil had finished all this tempting, he left him until an opportune time.

Jesus returned to Galilee in the power of the Spirit, and news about him spread through the whole countryside. He taught in their synagogues, and everyone praised him (Luke 4:1-15).

Jesus taught that people should withdraw from food for some time and give themselves to fasting.

He set an example on this by withdrawing from food for forty days and forty nights. He thus carried out a complete fast for forty days, and thus left us an example that we should follow in His steps.

Let us follow in His steps.

Super Time: Saving Time And Teaching Time

NOW ONE OF THE PHARISEES invited Jesus to have dinner with him, so he went to the Pharisee's house and reclined at the table.

When a woman who had lived a sinful life in that town learned that Jesus was eating at the Pharisee's house, she brought an alabaster jar of perfume, and as she stood behind him at his feet weeping, she began to wet his feet with her tears. Then she wiped them with her hair, kissed them and poured perfume on them.

When the Pharisee who had invited him saw this, he said to himself, "If this man were a prophet, he would know who is touching him and what kind of woman she is - that she is a sinner."

Jesus answered him, "Simon, I have something to tell you." "Tell me teacher," he said,

"Two men owed money to a certain moneylender. One owed him five hundred denarii, and the other fifty. Neither of them had the money to pay him back, so he cancelled the debts of both. Now which of them will love him more?"

Simon replied, "I suppose the one who had the bigger debt cancelled."

You have judged correctly," Jesus said. Then he turned towards the woman and said to Simon, "Do you see this woman? I came into your house. You did not give me any water for my feet, but she wet my feet and wiped them with her hair. You did not give me a kiss but this woman from the time I entered, has not stopped kissing my feet. You did not put oil on my head, but she has poured perfume on my feet. Therefore, I tell you, her many sins have been forgiven – for she loved much. But he who has been forgiven little loves little."

Then Jesus said to her, "Your sins are forgiven."

The other guests began to say among themselves, "Who is this who even forgives sins?"

Jesus said to the woman, "Your faith has saved you; go in peace"(Luke 7:36-50).

The life of Jesus was thoroughly positive. He was not bound by dos and don'ts. He sought every opportunity to do good. He was not bothered by what people would say.

One of the Pharisees invited Jesus to have dinner with him. He accepted the invitation and went to the dinner. During that dinner, He saved a lost sinner and taught that Pharisee (who invited Him) and the other guest important lessons.

He was in control.

He saw an opportunity to do good. He took up the opportunity at once and made an eternal difference to the life at least one person.

May we too accept the invitations that are given to us and go there, not mainly to eat, but to save the lost. May we also use the unique opportunities that are provided by meal times to invite the lost and drive eternal truths into their hearts!

May the Lord help us not to run away from the lost but to go to them with the message of life!

Amen.

The Food Of Jesus: Doing God's Will To The Finish

THE PHARISEES HEARD that Jesus was gaining and baptizing more disciples than John, although in fact it was not Jesus who baptized, but his disciples. When the Lord learned of this, he left Judea and went back once more to Galilee.

Now he had to go through Samaria. So he came to a town in Samaria called Sychar, near the plot of ground Jacob had given to his son Joseph. Jacob's well was there, and Jesus, tired as he was from the journey, sat down by the well. It was about the sixth hour.

When a Samaritan woman came to draw water, Jesus said to her, "Will you give me a drink?" (His disciples had gone into the town to buy food.)

The Samaritan woman said to him, "You are a Jew and I am a Samaritan woman. How can you ask me for a drink?" (For Jews do not associate with Samaritans.)

Jesus answered her, "If you knew the gift of God and who it is that asks you for a drink, you would have asked him and he would have given you living water."

Sir, the woman said, "You have nothing to draw with and the well is deep, where can you get this living water? Are you greater than our *father Jacob, who gave us the well and drank from it himself, as did also his sons and his flocks and herds?"*

Jesus answered, *"Everyone who drinks this water will be thirsty again, but whoever drinks the water I give him will never thirst. Indeed, the water I give him will become in him a spring of water welling up to eternal life."*

The woman said to him, *"Sir, give me this water so that I won't get thirsty and have to keep coming here to draw water."*

He told her, *"Go, call your husband and come back."*

"I have no husband," she replied.

Jesus said, to her, *"You are right when you say you have no husband. The fact is, you have had five husbands, and the man you now have is not your husband. What you have just said is quite true."*

"Sir," the woman said, *"I can see that you are a prophet. Our fathers worshipped on this mountain, but you Jews claim that the place where we must worship is in Jerusalem."*

Jesus declared, *"Believe me, woman, a time is coming when you will worship the Father neither on this mountain nor in Jerusalem. You Samaritans worship what you do not know; we worship what we do know, for salvation is from the Jews. Yet a time is coming and has now come when the true worshippers will worship the Father in spirit and truth, for they are the kind of worshippers the Father seeks. God is spirit, and his worshippers must worship in spirit and in truth."*

The woman said, *"I know that Messiah (called Christ) is coming. When he comes, he will explain everything to us."*

Then Jesus declared, *"I who speak to you am he."*

Just then his disciples returned and were surprised to find him talking with a woman. But no-one asked, *"What do you want?"* or *"Why are you talking with her?"*

Then, leaving her water jar, the woman went back to the town and said to the people, "Come, see a man who told me everything I ever did. Could this be the Christ?" They came out of the town and made their way towards him.

Meanwhile his disciples urged him, "Rabbi, eat something." But he said to them, "I have food to eat you know nothing about."

His disciples said to each other, "Could someone have brought him food?"

"My food," said Jesus, "is to do the will of him who sent me and to finish his work. Do you not say, 'Four months more and then the harvest'? I tell you, open your eyes and look at the fields! They are ripe for harvest. Even now the reaper draws his wages, even now he harvests the crop for eternal life, so that the sower and the reaper may be glad together. Thus the saying 'One sows and another reaps' is true. I sent you to reap what you have not worked for. The others have done the hard work, and you have reaped the benefits of their labour" (John 4:1-38).

The Lord Jesus was truly human. He was tired and hungry and His disciples went to town to buy food. It would have been expected that He would sit there under the weight of His tiredness and hunger. He did not. He soon found a lost woman and broke all the social customs and soon gave her a place among the saints who will reign with Him in glory.

His pre-occupation with this woman made Him put aside His tiredness and hunger. All of His being – spirit, soul and body was caught up in the battle to save her. He gave up tiredness and hunger!

The disciples came back with food and urged Him to eat. He was not interested. He was preoccupied with something greater than food. He was pre-occupied with doing and finishing the work of His father. He said, "My food is to do the will of him who sent me and to finish his work."

Many people have made food their reason for living. Jesus' reason for living and, consequently, His food was to do the will of His Father and to finish His work.

He was tired but He was not ruled by tiredness.

He was hungry but He was not ruled by hunger.

More than anyone else, He exemplified what the Apostle Paul wrote, *Everything is permissible for me" – but I will not be mastered by anything* (1 Corinthians 6:12).

Tiredness was permissible for the Lord Jesus, but He refused to be mastered by it. He put it aside at will and ministered life.

Hunger was permissible for the Lord Jesus, but He refused to be mastered by it. As the need arose, He put away hunger without satisfying it and gave Himself to the salvation of a woman and the multitude that followed her to Him.

He was really in control.

Food was good but it was only a means to an end. It was only useful if it helped the one who ate it to do the will of the father and finish the work the Father gave him.

He did not see food as a source of pleasure,

Enjoyment,

Power,

Glory,

and other self gratifying things of this life.

He saw it as a tool to help Him to do the will of His Father and finish His Father's work.

He saw food as useful but not indispensable at moments when there was a greater work to do than feed the body.

He made food a servant and caused food to remain a servant.

DELIVERANCE FROM THE SIN OF GLUTTONY

He never made any room for food to become a master.

He could be hungry and yet say "No" to the offer of food.

He was in supreme control.

Glory be to God.

You too can know the secret of His authority and enter and walk in it!

Amen.

Deliverance From The Sin Of Gluttony

A Necessity – 1: The Idol Must Be Overthrown

Because gluttony is the overthrow of God and the enthronement of food on the heart, it is imperative that food be taken out of the heart and the Lord God Almighty be enthroned.

The hymn writer puts it in the following words:

The dearest idol I have ever known
Whatever that idol be
Help me to tear it from Thy throne
And worship only Thee. (SS and S No. 583)

For the glutton, food is his idol.

This idol must be removed from the heart at all costs.

The Lord God Almighty must be enthroned therein.

The obedience that was hitherto given to the idol —food, must now be given exclusively to the Lord God Almighty.

Food must be given its rightful place of a servant and allowed to serve when the need arises.

A Necessity – 2: Admit That You Are A

Glutton

NO ONE CAN BE SET FREE from gluttony unless he admits the fact that he is a glutton. If you are the one who says any of the following, then you are not ready to be delivered.

01. I eat little but I put on weight.
02. I have big bones, that is why I put on weight.
03. I am big because I inherited it from my ancestors.
04. I am fat because of indigestion.
05. I work in a place where I always see food that is why I eat much.
06. Every other excuse.

There is only one way through which weight enters the body – the mouth. What does not enter the mouth does not go down into the body.

You have been committing the sin of gluttony. If you do not admit it, then you are neither ready nor serious and there is nothing that anybody can do to help you. The Bible says: *If we claim to be without sin, we deceive ourselves and the truth is not in us. If we confess our sins, he is faithful and just and will forgive us our sins and purify us from all unrighteousness* (1 John 1: 8-9).

Why not confess to the Lord God Almighty telling Him: My Lord, I, Professor, Reverend, Pastor, Mr, Mrs, Miss ....am a glutton and I have been practicing gluttony.

A Necessity – 3: Admit That You Cannot Set Yourself Free

IF YOU ARE HONEST, you will admit that you have tried hard to deliver yourself – you have tried this diet and the other; you have lost so many kilos and time only to recover them and even add more.

You have tried very hard but failed lamentably. You had taken the resolutions not to overeat but each time you saw food you forgot your resolutions and remembered them only after committing the sin.

Tell the Lord, "I cannot deliver myself."

A Necessity – 4: Invite The Holy Spirit To Be Your Deliverer

ALL ALONG, YOU HAVE tried to set yourself free and failed lamentably. You have even prayed and fasted, yet you are still bound. The truth is that in your flesh, there is nothing that can deliver you.

Your will

Your mind

Your emotions

are all part of your flesh. They cannot deliver you from the flesh because flesh cannot deliver flesh from flesh.

The Holy Spirit is the Representative of the Lord Jesus in you. He is mighty and powerful. He can do all things. He can do anything. He can do what the flesh could not do. If you hand over to the Holy Spirit the task of delivering you from gluttony, He will take over and do an excellent job.

If you want to invite Him to become your deliverer pray and tell him: "Blessed Holy Spirit, You are the Representative of the Lord Jesus in me. You are the Almighty. You are able to do everything you decide to do. I have tried to deliver myself from gluttony in vain. I have failed many times. If I were to try again, I would fail again. I have stopped trying. I plead with you to take over and deliver me completely from gluttony that I may be delivered once for all. Take over from this moment and do that which you alone can do. I will not stand on your way. I will not resist you. I will obey all your commands while I follow, O Mighty Deliverer. Because I have handed everything into your hands and because of your power and your willingness to deliver, I consider myself delivered from gluttony now and henceforth, I will walk in the power of the Holy Spirit in the life of the delivered. Thank you Holy Spirit for setting me free from gluttony. Thank you, because I am now free and by your strength, not mine, I will remain delivered forever. The uncontrollable desire for food is gone. Henceforth, I will eat under the personal leading of the Holy Spirit. I will eat what He commands me to eat. I will stop eating once He sounds the whistle saying that I have eaten enough. Excess kilograms will begin to disappear, I am free, free, free. I bless the Lord Jesus for the Holy Spirit who has set me free.

Glory be to the Lord God Almighty! Amen.

A Necessity – 5: Walking By The Spirit Minute By Minute

THE BIBLE SAYS: ...*live by the Spirit, and you will not gratify the desires of the sinful nature* (Galatians 5:16).

What does it mean by living by the Spirit? It means the following things among many others:

1) You will ask the Holy Spirit to fill you to overflowing as many times as possible every day. Do it a thousand times if possible. Ask him to fill you to overflowing and to possess your whole being at all times. Every time you ask Him to fill you and to possess you, consecrate your all anew to Him.

2) Continue to depend 100% on him alone, as your Deliverer. Do not turn away from Him and turn towards your own thoughts, your will or your emotions such that you begin to set your own laws on how to remain delivered. You began in the Holy Spirit. If you turn towards the flesh to continue that which started in the Holy Spirit, you would be surprised by how soon you will fail. The flesh counts for nothing.

3) Whatever the Holy Spirit will ask you to do ask Him to give you power to do it. He will immediately give you power to do it and you will do it by His strength. For example, when you will have eaten only 50% of the quantity of food you ate in the past, you would hear His voice asking you to stop because you have had enough. Say to Him immediately: "Lord, you are right. I have had enough. Give me the power to stop right now." Immediately after your prayer, His power will come upon you at once and deliver you from the desire to eat more. Move away immediately from the food and do not try to take another spoon. You must obey Him

immediately. If you are eating a carrot and He blows the whistle to announce that you have had enough of it, stop eating at once and put away the remaining piece. Do not decide to disobey Him by finishing the remaining piece of carrot. The walk with the Holy Spirit requires that He be obeyed immediately. He will not accept delayed obedience. Once you begin to render him implicit obedience in all things, His voice will become clearer and clearer and your deliverance from gluttony will become more and more visible. Excess kilograms will begin to disappear and your strength will begin to be renewed. You will receive increasing physical and spiritual strength and a song of praise will become frequent on your lips.

4) He will begin to show you other domains of your life apart from that of food and feeding habits which need to be subjected to His leading. Just obey as He leads. Continue and continue with Him.

5) You have been delivered from gluttony. You are delivered. You have been delivered from other chains.

6) Praise the Lord!

Amen.

Don't miss out!

Visit the website below and you can sign up to receive emails whenever Zacharias Tanee Fomum publishes a new book. There's no charge and no obligation.

https://books2read.com/r/B-A-CKEB-ROQAB

BOOKS 2 READ

Connecting independent readers to independent writers.

Did you love *Deliverance From The Sin of Gluttony*? Then you should read *Deliverance From Sin* by Zacharias Tanee Fomum!

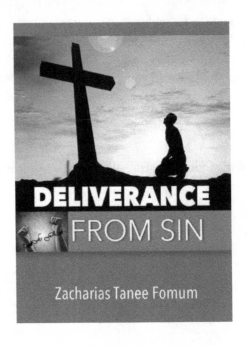

Although the five books are complementary and help the reader to have a more complete view of the theme, each book is complete in its own right and should be read for the profit of it.Although the books are rooted in the Word of God, they are written, not merely to help readers to know God's point of view about the matters discussed, but also to lead the believer beyond theoretical understanding into spiritual experience; for sanctification is, ultimately, not merely a doctrine but an experience. My prayer for you is that the One who Achose us in Him, before the foundation of the world, that we should be holy and blameless before him" (Ephesians 1:4), should work mightily in you as you read, working in you and through you, so that you may enter into and make progress in the life of sanctification.God bless you exceedingly.

Read more at www.ztfbooks.com.

About the Author

ZACHARIAS TANEE FOMUM is the bestselling author of more than 500 books with over 10 million copies in print. He founded **Christian Missionary Fellowship International** (CMFI), a missionary movement that has planted thousands of churches in more than 105 nations on all continents.

Zacharias was also a **professor of Organic Chemistry** with more than 160 publications in leading international journals. In 2005, his published scientific work was evaluated and found to be of high distinction, earning him the award of a Doctor of Science degree from the University of Durham, Great Britain.

Prof. Fomum was **married to Prisca and their seven children** are actively involved with missionary and church planting work across the globe.

His books and the millions of people he influenced in **more than 40 years of Christian ministry** continue to impact the world with the Gospel today!

Read more at www.ztfbooks.com.

CPSIA information can be obtained
at www.ICGtesting.com
Printed in the USA
BVHW071535070421
604343BV00006B/910

9 781393 104780